# 52 WEEKS

OSCAR C. JOHNSON PHD

*52 Weeks*

Copyright © 2021 by *Oscar C. Johnson PhD*

All rights reserved. No part of this publication may be reproduced, distributed, or transmitted in any form or by any means, including photocopying, recording, or other electronic or mechanical methods, without the prior written permission of the author, except in the case of brief quotations embodied in critical reviews and certain other non-commercial uses permitted by copyright law.

ISBN
978-1-956529-28-9 (Paperback)
978-1-956529-27-2 (eBook)

# PREFACE

52 weeks is a book of scripture topic meditation. Unlike a daily verse to read, it focuses on the same topic for a week. The intent is to get to know that topic much better as it directs us to look at multiple verses and conversations in the Bible about a particular topic. It frequently will present a topic from the viewpoint of different authors.

There is nothing special about who I am. I consider myself an average Christian with a strong belief and trust in God. I am not a gifted speaker, nor have I ever written anything other than college papers and a few science articles. I pray and read scripture daily to start my day and give me something to reflect on during the day.

When I started this book, I wanted to give the reader something to focus on for more than one day. I found that studying one topic for a week gave me a greater insight to that topic and made it more pertinent to my life. In writing this book, I found that I studied more deeply than I did with daily scripture topics.

I don't consider myself a great writer as I said, I'm pretty much an average guy. I'm not a philosopher or a deep thinker by any standard. That being the case, this book is relatively superficial. It addresses my feelings toward a subject. It may or may not be in line with the great religious thinkers, but it is how I interpret the various topics in this book.

We all have gifts given to us by God that we use to spread the gospel. I hope that this book reaches those who want to understand and seek more knowledge about the message of God. I believe that the Lord has helped me to write this book to spread his Word. I pray that it will help bring one closer to God. It continues to help me.

# Table of Contents

Forgiveness ................................................................ 1
Happiness ................................................................ 13
Faith ...................................................................... 25
Salvation ................................................................ 37
Sin ........................................................................ 45
Assurance .............................................................. 53
The Bible ............................................................... 61
Blessed .................................................................. 69
Jesus ..................................................................... 79
Children ................................................................ 89
Christian Living ..................................................... 97
The Church ......................................................... 105
Comfort ............................................................... 113
Death ................................................................... 121
Disobedience ....................................................... 129
Doubt .................................................................. 139
Giving .................................................................. 147
God's Care .......................................................... 155
God's Will ........................................................... 163
Grace ................................................................... 171
Heaven ................................................................ 181
Holy Spirit .......................................................... 189
Humility .............................................................. 197
Justice .................................................................. 205
Love ..................................................................... 213

| | |
|---|---|
| Praise | 223 |
| Prayer | 233 |
| Preaching | 241 |
| Resurrection | 249 |
| Sanctification | 257 |
| Second Coming | 265 |
| Patience | 273 |
| Wisdom | 281 |
| Works | 289 |
| Worldliness | 299 |
| Taming The Tongue | 307 |
| Suffering And Presecution | 315 |
| Natural Disasters | 323 |
| Managing Time | 331 |
| Overcoming Prejudice | 339 |
| Pride | 347 |
| God's Help | 355 |
| Seeking Strength | 363 |
| Anger | 371 |
| Discouraged | 379 |
| Belief | 387 |
| Fear | 395 |
| Relationship With God | 403 |
| Relationships With Others | 411 |
| Temptation | 419 |
| Parables | 427 |
| About Hell | 435 |

# WEEK 1
# FORGIVENESS

DAY 1
SUGGESTED READING
JOHN 1:29

> **²⁹ The next day John seeth Jesus coming unto him, and saith, Behold the Lamb of God, which taketh away the sin of the world. (KJV)**

John the Baptist saw Jesus coming and announces him to the world as the one to take away all sin.

The implication of this proclamation cannot be understated. Jesus has the ability to take away all sin. This gives one who believes a reset of their life from one of sinful damnation to one of righteous salvation. This gift from God is the greatest of his gifts.

Don't be confused though, this does not mean you won't sin again. Chances are you will. God does promise that if you confess your sins and repent through Jesus's name, he will forgive you. This appears to be a pass to sin freely but what really happens after accepting Christ is a building of ones' spirit to avoid what is unrighteous.

So think about this, repent and confess to Jesus. Do this immediately if you can. Learn from your sin. God is patient and will forgive.

*DAY 2*
*SUGGESTED READING*
*LUKE 15:18 – 24*

**¹⁸ I will set out and go back to my father and say to him: Father, I have sinned against heaven and against you.**

**¹⁹ I am no longer worthy to be called your son; make me like one of your hired servants.'**

**²⁰ So he got up and went to his father.**

**"But while he was still a long way off, his father saw him and was filled with compassion for him; he ran to his son, threw his arms around him and kissed him.**

**²¹ "The son said to him, 'Father, I have sinned against heaven and against you. I am no longer worthy to be called your son.'**

**²² "But the father said to his servants, 'Quick! Bring the best robe and put it on him. Put a ring on his finger and sandals on his feet.**

**²³ Bring the fattened calf and kill it. Let's have a feast and celebrate.**

**²⁴ For this son of mine was dead and is alive again; he was lost and is found.' So they began to celebrate. (NIV)**

In the story of the prodigal son, Jesus tells us of an ungrateful son who squandered his money and lived an immoral and sinful life. When he realized the wrongness of his ways, he returned to his father full of remorse and wanting to repent. He felt he did not deserve his place in the family, but his father was overjoyed with his return and stated, "For this son of mine was dead and is alive again; he was lost and is found". (Luke 15:24 NIV)

This is the life of many Christians. For whenever our lives get derailed and we abandon the life of Christ, we become a servant of sin.

However, God forgives like the father in this parable. He rejoices when one of his children returns to the ways of righteousness. God accepts you back through an unearned and underserved concept call grace. The amazing thing is that, chances are, you are unworthy of this grace. Fortunately, God does not base his relationship with you on your worthiness. He accepts you solely on the basis of his infinite love.

*DAY 3*
*SUGGESTED READING*
*LUKE 6:27 – 36*

[27] "**But to you who are listening I say: Love your enemies, do good to those who hate you,**

[28] **bless those who curse you, pray for those who mistreat you.**

[29] **If someone slaps you on one cheek, turn to them the other also. If someone takes your coat, do not withhold your shirt from them.**

[30] **Give to everyone who asks you, and if anyone takes what belongs to you, do not demand it back.**

[31] **Do to others as you would have them do to you.**

[32] "**If you love those who love you, what credit is that to you? Even sinners love those who love them.**

[33] **And if you do good to those who are good to you, what credit is that to you? Even sinners do that.**

[34] **And if you lend to those from whom you expect repayment, what credit is that to you? Even sinners lend to sinners, expecting to be repaid in full.**

**³⁵ But love your enemies, do good to them, and lend to them without expecting to get anything back. Then your reward will be great, and you will be children of the Most High, because he is kind to the ungrateful and wicked.**

**³⁶ Be merciful, just as your Father is merciful. (NIV)**

Today we contemplate on something that we as Christians have all said or thought; "I can never forgive him/her". A statement like this is typically fueled by an emotionally laden event. Satan uses emotions to allow hate, anger, jealously, envy pain and any other negative feelings to persistently linger. The feelings of resentment fail to go away.

This is not unanticipated though. When feelings are involved faith takes a back seat. Feelings are subject to man's, and more importantly, Satan's whims. Therefore, feelings can be manipulated. In this scenario, we can forgive but typically will not forget.

To truly forgive one must rely on faith. True forgiveness has nothing to do with how one feels. It is an act of will. It is based on prayer and having faith that the prayer has been answered.

Once you have forgiven by prayer, you must forgive as God does. He forgives and forgets. When Satan tries to rekindle old memories, remember they are forgiven by faith, not feelings. The resentment is now permanently and unconditionally removed, and you spirit will be at ease.

*DAY 4*
*SUGGESTED READING*
*1 JOHN 1:9*

**⁹ If we confess our sins, he is faithful and just to forgive us our sins, and to cleanse us from all unrighteousness. (KJV)**

Sometimes we are so busy in our lives we are not aware of the fact we are sinning. This may be due to distraction or an inadvertency. Other times we willfully sin. Regardless of the situation, we as Christians will eventually realize we had sinned.

Most of the time we pray for forgiveness and move forward. However, may times we forget to repent and our sins start to stack upon themselves. After a while fear and guilt pushes us farther from God. This is a perfect scenario for Satan, as he will insidiously plant thoughts of helplessness in our minds.

But John reaffirms God's promise to us. It doesn't matter how much we have sinned. We just need to repent and confess to reestablish our relationship with God. God knows when you are feeling guilty. He knows you are sorry. Therefore, he gave his son, Jesus Christ, to wash our sins anyway with his blood and mediate between us and the Father, God, for forgiveness.

No matter how bad the sin or how long since one has repented, seek God. He wants to forgive and ease your soul.

DAY 5
SUGGESTED READING
PSALM 103:1 – 12

¹ Bless the LORD, O my soul: and all that is within me, bless his holy name.

² Bless the LORD, O my soul, and forget not all his benefits:

³ Who forgiveth all thine iniquities; who healeth all thy diseases;

⁴ Who redeemeth thy life from destruction; who crowneth thee with lovingkindness and tender mercies;

⁵ Who satisfieth thy mouth with good things; so that thy youth is renewed like the eagle's.

⁶ The LORD executeth righteousness and judgment for all that are oppressed.

⁷ He made known his ways unto Moses, his acts unto the children of Israel.

⁸ The LORD is merciful and gracious, slow to anger, and plenteous in mercy.

⁹ He will not always chide: neither will he keep his anger forever.

**¹⁰ He hath not dealt with us after our sins; nor rewarded us according to our iniquities.**

**¹¹ For as the heaven is high above the earth, so great is his mercy toward them that fear him.**

**¹² As far as the east is from the west, so far hath he removed our transgressions from us. (KJV)**

Sin is like debt. If unrepented it builds to a point where we believe it cannot be repaid. This couldn't be farther from the truth. We fail to ask for forgiveness because we are afraid of what God will do or we don't care one way or the other.

David explains God's capacity for forgiveness in Psalm 103. In it, he explains that God's capacity to forgive is vast; "as far as the east is from the west, so far has he removed our transgressions from us". (Psalms 103:12 NIV) We can't compile enough sin that he would not forgive.

He forgives our total debt and then forgets. His mercy is limitless. How great is God that we can start anew?

DAY 6
SUGGESTED READING
ISAIAH 1:18

> **¹⁸ Come now, and let us reason together, saith the LORD: though your sins be as scarlet, they shall be as white as snow; though they be red like crimson, they shall be as wool. (KJV)**

There was an insect that produced bright red dye from its eggs. This dye fixed to cloth and could not be washed out. Isaiah likened this red dye to sin because sin could not be removed. Sin permeates every fiber of our being. It is in our heart and soul. There is nothing man can do to remove it.

Only God can cleanse man from sin. He tells us he will "they shall be as white as snow". (Isaiah 1:18 NIV) A millennium later, Peter confirms this; "repent, then, and turn to God, so that he will forgive your sins. (Acts 3:19 GNT)

This is the promise of God to remove the blemish of sin from us, permanently.

DAY 7
SUGGESTED READING
ROMANS 6:23

## ²³ For the wages of sin is death; but the gift of God is eternal life through Jesus Christ our Lord. (KJV)

"The wages of sin is death" (Romans 6:23 KJV). This concept originated before the sin actually occurred as God told Adam "of the tree of the knowledge of Good and Evil you shall not eat. For in that day you eat of it you will surely die". (Genesis 2:17 KJV)

Now we recognize this death as the result of the original sin committed by Eve, then Adam. The first death was to animals, from which God took their furs to make clothes for Adan and Eve, and then to man.

Now the Lord says; "for all have sinned and fall short of the glory of God" (Romans 3:23 NIV). That is everyone.

Then God gives us the gift. He gives us the gift of eternal life through his son. This is the ultimate act of forgiveness and love from God.

# WEEK 2
# HAPPINESS

DAY 1
SUGGESTED READING
PSALM 1:1 -3

**¹ Blessed is the man that walketh not in the counsel of the ungodly, nor standeth in the way of sinners, nor sitteth in the seat of the scornful.**

**² But his delight is in the law of the Lord; and in his law doth he meditate day and night.**

**³ And he shall be like a tree planted by the rivers of water, that bringeth forth his fruit in his season; his leaf also shall not wither; and whatsoever he doeth shall prosper. (KJV)**

When I think of what makes me happy as a Christian, I always refer to the Psalms of David. They will lift my spirit and reaffirm the promises of God.

In his first Psalm, David reflects on those who enjoy obeying the Law of the Lord. We need to think about this with regard to our own behavior.

*DAY 2*
*SUGGESTED READING*
*PSALM 89:15 – 18*

**¹⁵ Blessed is the people that know the joyful sound: they shall walk, O LORD, in the light of thy countenance.**

**¹⁶ In thy name shall they rejoice all the day: and in thy righteousness shall they be exalted.**

**¹⁷ For thou art the glory of their strength: and in thy favour our horn shall be exalted.**

**¹⁸ For the LORD is our defence; and the Holy One of Israel is our king. (KJV)**

There are times that we are so happy that we sing our praises to the Lord. These praises are the blessings and triumphants that you have provided us. The praises are for the just laws for which we obey. The praises are for our savior, Jesus Christ.

Think about everything we have overcome. Think about every triumph in our lives and you will want to sing his praises also.

DAY 3
SUGGESTED READING
PSALM 19:7 – 11

**⁷ The law of the L**ORD** is perfect, converting the soul: the testimony of the L**ORD** is sure, making wise the simple.**

**⁸ The statutes of the L**ORD** are right, rejoicing the heart: the commandment of the L**ORD** is pure, enlightening the eyes.**

**⁹ The fear of the L**ORD** is clean, enduring for ever: the judgments of the L**ORD** are true and righteous altogether.**

**¹⁰ More to be desired are they than gold, yea, than much fine gold: sweeter also than honey and the honeycomb.**

**¹¹ Moreover by them is thy servant warned: and in keeping of them there is great reward. (KJV)**

Observing children, I see that they seem to be the happiest when they have structure. Their frustrations occur when they limit test and are corrected or chastised. Eventually, they will understand the rules and limits and then they are at peace.

Christians are the children of God. He has given us his laws and those that obey them are at peace and happy. We must meditate on his laws day and night to protect us from the corruptibility of the world. It is our steadfastness to obedience of the Law that we are rewarded by the Father, Almighty.

*DAY 4*
*SUGGESTED READING*
*PSALM 23:1 – 8*

¹ **The Lord is my shepherd; I shall not want.**

² **He maketh me to lie down in green pastures: he leadeth me beside the still waters.**

³ **He restoreth my soul: he leadeth me in the paths of righteousness for his name's sake.**

⁴ **Yea, though I walk through the valley of the shadow of death, I will fear no evil: for thou art with me; thy rod and thy staff they comfort me.**

⁵ **Thou preparest a table before me in the presence of mine enemies: thou anointest my head with oil; my cup runneth over.**

⁶ **Surely goodness and mercy shall follow me all the days of my life: and I will dwell in the house of the Lord forever. (KJV)**

In this psalm we need to realize the happiness of David. He obviously is happy that God is his provider and protector.

In our lives, doesn't God also provide and protect us? He does this on a daily basis. For this, we should rely on him heavily.

The last portion of this psalm, proclaims God promise to us of prosperity and his love.

DAY 5
SUGGESTED READING
PSALM 119:1 – 8

> <sup>1</sup> **Happy are those whose lives are faultless,
> who live according to the law of the L**ORD**.**
>
> <sup>2</sup> **Happy are those who follow his commands,
> who obey him with all their heart.**
>
> <sup>3</sup> **They never do wrong;
> they walk in the L**ORD**'s ways.**
>
> <sup>4</sup> **L**ORD**, you have given us your laws
> and told us to obey them faithfully.**
>
> <sup>5</sup> **How I hope that I shall be faithful
> in keeping your instructions!**
>
> <sup>6</sup> **If I pay attention to all your commands,
> then I will not be put to shame.**
>
> <sup>7</sup> **As I learn your righteous judgments,
> I will praise you with a pure heart.**
>
> <sup>8</sup> **I will obey your laws;
> never abandon me! (GNT)**

As Christians, we should always be aware of the Laws of the Lord. Obedience of the laws are what makes us happy in our lives. The Christian knows that they have are not at liberty to divide their heart between God and Satan. Through belief of God's promises we are happy. This is as it should be though.

The Christian life is fulfilled when it is faultless. The soul must be committed to the Lord only and not the world because we cannot serve two masters.

Monitor yourself constantly. Not only your actions but your thoughts. Repent if you sin immediately. It only takes a moment to step back and get in touch with God.

The Lord wants us to be happy. He is always there for us. Don't risk everlasting shame through disobedience.

DAY 6
SUGGESTED READING
PSALM 119:49 – 56

> [49] Remember your promise to me, your servant;
> it has given me hope.
>
> [50] Even in my suffering I was comforted
> because your promise gave me life.
>
> [51] The proud are always scornful of me,
> but I have not departed from your law.
>
> [52] I remember your judgments of long ago,
> and they bring me comfort, O LORD.
>
> [53] When I see the wicked breaking your law,
> I am filled with anger.
>
> [54] During my brief earthly life
> I compose songs about your commands.
>
> [55] In the night I remember you, LORD,
> and I think about your law.
>
> [56] I find my happiness
> in obeying your commands. (GNT)

As we go through our lives, we can be relieved that God has promised us relief from worldly evil. God will give us comfort during times of trouble.

There will be those who insult us and tempt us to do evil, but we must persevere as sin is horrid to us.

Always remember the Word of God. Study it and use it as a shield. In the end, the Law of the Lord will make us happy with the knowledge that we will always prevail.

Think of all the promises that God has made throughout the Bible.

*Oscar C. Johnson PhD*

*DAY 7*
*SUGGESTED READING*
*MATTHEW 5:3 – 12*

³ "**Happy are those who know they are spiritually poor;**
the Kingdom of heaven belongs to them!

⁴ "**Happy are those who mourn;**
God will comfort them!

⁵ "**Happy are those who are humble;**
they will receive what God has promised!

⁶ "**Happy are those whose greatest desire is to do what God requires;**
God will satisfy them fully!

⁷ "**Happy are those who are merciful to others;**
God will be merciful to them!

⁸ "**Happy are the pure in heart;**
they will see God!

⁹ "**Happy are those who work for peace;**
God will call them his children!

¹⁰ "**Happy are those who are persecuted because they do what God requires;**
the Kingdom of heaven belongs to them!

¹¹ "**Happy are you when people insult you and**

**persecute you and tell all kinds of evil lies against you because you are my followers.**

**¹² Be happy and glad, for a great reward is kept for you in heaven. This is how the prophets who lived before you were persecuted. (GNT)**

The Beautitudes are the expression of true happiness. The Greek word translated "blessed" means "happy, blissful" or, literally, "to be enlarged."

When Jesus started the Sermon of the Mount, he was saying "divinely happy and fortunate are" those who possess these inward qualities. These are the same qualities that Jesus demonstrated and expects them of us as Christians.

Each saying speaks of a blessing or "divine favor" bestowed upon a person resulting from the possession of a certain character quality. The person whom Jesus describes in this passage has a different quality of character and lifestyle than those still unsaved.

Jesus teaches us that if we live according to the Beatitudes, we will live a happy Christian life. The Beatitudes fulfill God's promises made to Abraham and his descendants and describe the rewards that will be ours as loyal followers of Christ.

# WEEK 3
# FAITH

DAY 1
SUGGESTED READING
HEBREW 11:1 – 39

> **¹ To have faith is to be sure of the things we hope for, to be certain of the things we cannot see.**
>
> **² It was by their faith that people of ancient times won God's approval.**
>
> **³ It is by faith that we understand that the universe was created by God's word, so that what can be seen was made out of what cannot be seen.**
>
> **⁶ No one can please God without faith, for whoever comes to God must have faith that God exists and rewards those who seek him. (GNT)**

As a scientist, I have been trained to believe in certain ways. My training says something is true when it can be tested and then tested again to get the same results. That is scientific faith.

Biblical faith does not follow these rules. It requires one to realize an unrealistic concept of hope to be a reality. This reality is based on another faith: God exist. If you believe this, then you accept some essential truths about God:

- He is completely sovereign
- He is infinite in wisdom
- He is perfect in love

In Jerry Bridges book, *Trusting God*, he sums up these statements in an anonymous quote; "God in his love always wills what is best for us, in his wisdom he always knows what is best, and in his sovereignty, he has the power to bring it about".

Faith is not a promise of hope. It is a statement of fact. Faith works because Jesus and God never change.

DAY 2
SUGGESTED READING
ROMANS 3:27 – 28

**²⁷ Where is boasting then? It is excluded. By what law? of works? Nay: but by the law of faith.**

**²⁸ Therefore we conclude that a man is justified by faith without the deeds of the law. (KJV)**

Paul tells the Romans that only faith is required to be justified in Christs' eyes. There is no requirement of "works" less someone will boast. If a person could be saved by "works" then faith would not be necessary. One would only need to keep track of their works and then bargain with God for salvation. He could also bargain for other things like health, happiness, wealth or influence.

There is no place for boasting in the heart of a Christian. It is by grace that we are saved. Grace from faith excludes all boasting.

DAY 3
SUGGESTED READING
Mark 11:22 – 24

**²² And Jesus answering saith unto them, Have faith in God.**

**²³ For verily I say unto you, That whosoever shall say unto this mountain, Be thou removed, and be thou cast into the sea; and shall not doubt in his heart, but shall believe that those things which he saith shall come to pass; he shall have whatsoever he saith.**

**²⁴ Therefore I say unto you, What things soever ye desire, when ye pray, believe that ye receive them, and ye shall have them. (KJV)**

When we think of faith, are we having faith in the Holy Spirit, Jesus or God? In these passages, Jesus says have faith in God. Because of this faith and ones' belief, your prayers will be answered.

What needs to be contemplated here is the fact that there are significant issues in our lives that need intervention by God. By faith, God will solve problems for us. He can overcome any obstacle disrupting one's life.

Answered prayer is a free gift of God. We do not know Gods' plan, so we cannot know if our prayer fits into his larger scheme. To please God, we must have faith. The best we can do is believe that our prayer is answered and wait patiently. Trust in Gods' mercy that he will answer it.

*DAY 4*
*SUGGESTED READING*
*ROMANS 10:17*

**$^{17}$ Consequently, faith comes from hearing the message, and the message is heard through the word about Christ. (NIV)**

Faith involves believing what God says and that what He says is completely trustworthy. Faith is an assurance as stated in Hebrews 11. It is a conviction of things that we have not seen. Without faith it is impossible to please God.

It is by faith that salvation is attained. The faith that saves is not of human origin, but it is a gift of God. It doesn't come from me or from anyone else however faith can be strengthened by the hearing the Word of God.

We must constantly read the Bible. We must be attentive at church and in bible study. The more we do these things the stronger our faith will be. Jesus says in John 15:4 (NIV), "Abide in me and I in you".

*DAY 5*
*SUGGESTED READING*
*ROMANS 10:10*

**¹⁰ For it is with your heart that you believe and are justified, and it is with your mouth that you profess your faith and are saved. (NIV)**

So, who has faith? The Bible tells us we have faith if we confess our sins to Jesus. If we believe that he died for our sins and that God raised him from the dead.

Faith is part of God's plan of justifying people. One who believes through faith is righteous in God's eyes. Their sins can now be pardoned as they become one of God's children.

Confession is also part of the plan. Those who confess or profess their attachment to Christ shall be saved. No matter the persecution or opposition, the Christian will stay true to his confession in Christ.

DAY 6
SUGGESTED READING
MATTHEW 7:7 – 11

> **⁷ "Ask and it will be given to you; seek and you will find; knock and the door will be opened to you.**
>
> **⁸ For everyone who asks receives; the one who seeks finds; and to the one who knocks, the door will be opened.**
>
> **⁹ "Which of you, if your son asks for bread, will give him a stone?**
>
> **¹⁰ Or if he asks for a fish, will give him a snake?**
>
> **¹¹ If you, then, though you are evil, know how to give good gifts to your children, how much more will your Father in heaven give good gifts to those who ask him! (NIV)**

Most people have heard the expression, "Ask, and you shall receive, Seek, and you shall find and Knock, and the door will be opened to you". Most people don't know that it is from the Bible.

These verses have a hidden meaning for me. I think of when I was not a Christian and first heard them. I asked about Christ. I sought more knowledge about Christ. The door was opened, and Christ accepted me.

The message is one of faith. We must trust our Almighty Father to provide for us when we are seeking help. As explained, any father would give good things to his children. Their children never question their father's act. Would God do any less for his children?

Prayer is the appointed means for obtaining what we need. Pray; pray often; make a habit of prayer and be serious and earnest in it. If your prayer fits into God's plan, then he will answer it. This applies to any Christian.

DAY 7
SUGGESTED READING
JOHN 20:24 – 29

²⁴ But Thomas, one of the twelve, called Didymus, was not with them when Jesus came.

²⁵ The other disciples therefore said unto him, We have seen the LORD. But he said unto them, Except I shall see in his hands the print of the nails, and put my finger into the print of the nails, and thrust my hand into his side, I will not believe.

²⁶ And after eight days again his disciples were within, and Thomas with them: then came Jesus, the doors being shut, and stood in the midst, and said, Peace be unto you.

²⁷ Then saith he to Thomas, Reach hither thy finger, and behold my hands; and reach hither thy hand, and thrust it into my side: and be not faithless, but believing.

²⁸ And Thomas answered and said unto him, My LORD and my God.

²⁹ Jesus saith unto him, Thomas, because thou hast seen me, thou hast believed: blessed are they that have not seen, and yet have believed. (KJV)

Everyone knows what a Doubting Thomas is. They, of course, are people who do not believe in something until they see it themselves. There are many people in the world like that today. This can be justified with all the evil and deception that exist. Whenever something is presented to you consider the source. The world of man is treacherous.

The original Doubting Thomas did not believe his fellow disciples when then told they told him that Christ had risen from the grave and they had seen him. Thomas had lost touch with his brothers and faith waned as a result. Jesus later appeared to him and told him to stop doubting. He then mentioned the faith of those who believe in him without seeing him. Keeping the right company too is critical for the Christian life.

# WEEK 4
# SALVATION

*DAY 1*
*SUGGESTED READING*
*JOHN 3:16-17*

**[16] For God so loved the world, that he gave his only begotten Son, that whosoever believeth in him should not perish, but have everlasting life.**

**[17] For God sent not his Son into the world to condemn the world; but that the world through him might be saved. (KJV)**

This passage is seen at almost every sporting event that is televised. Someone in the stands is supporting a homemade sign that sends this message. Though most people know the verses, they really are not truly aware of what is being conveyed.

The world is in a condemned state and though God loved the sinners, he hated the sin. Despite man's wickedness, God through benevolence, gave the world his son as a means of redemption.

The salvation is not without a price. Understanding what God and Jesus require of this salvation is paramount to the message of the New Testament.

DAY 2
SUGGESTED READING
ACTS 4:12

**Salvation is found in no one else, for there is no other name under heaven given to mankind by which we must be saved. (KJV)**

No person can be saved except through Jesus Christ. There is a fundamental acceptance that must be in place for salvation to occur. This is established in belief in Jesus's gospel.

When Peter made this declaration, he wanted the Jewish leaders to understand that Jesus was the one spoken of in scripture and his teachings were unique. He makes it clear that Jesus and his message is from God.

Though this message was primarily to address the Jews, the message is doubtless for Gentiles also. For Jesus's gospel is intended to save all people from death and the fire of hell.

*DAY 3*
*SUGGESTED READING*
*ROMANS 10:9 - 10*

**⁹ If you confess that Jesus is Lord and believe that God raised him from death, you will be saved.**

**¹⁰ For it is by our faith that we are put right with God; it is by our confession that we are saved. (GNT)**

There are many good people that accept the fact that there is a God and that Jesus is his son. They think that this belief is enough to allow them a place in heaven.

They could be no farther from the truth. Though these people may be righteous, they are not realizing that salvation requires more than acknowledgement of God and Jesus.

The study of Romans explores all facets of sin and salvation. Explore this message that Paul brings the Romans.

*DAY 4*
*SUGGESTED READING*
*EPHESIANS 2:8 – 9*

**⁸ For by grace are ye saved through faith; and that not of yourselves: it is the gift of God:**

**⁹ Not of works, lest any man should boast. (KJV)**

These two verses are elegant in their simplicity. They are easily understood for anyone. However, they are more complex than what is being so simply stated.

Understand that grace is the gift. Grace does not require an act. Faith alone is all that is required. Therefore, salvation is given for free. How many are those who think that all the great contributions they have made for the good of others is enough to warrant salvation? They do not understand how God's love works.

Those who are seeking salvation know, by now, that they are sinners and spiritually dead in the eyes of God. Nonetheless, God's love is constant, and he provided a way back to him. This is through his son Jesus Christ.

DAY 5
SUGGESTED READING
MATTHEW 7:13 - 14

**[13] "Enter through the narrow gate. For wide is the gate and broad is the road that leads to destruction, and many enter through it.**

**[14] But small is the gate and narrow the road that leads to life, and only a few find it. (NIV)**

We are all taught to take the path of least resistance. Ockam's Razor is a principle that states; "The explanation requiring the fewest assumptions is most likely to be correct." This can also be interpreted as, "Keep it Simple".

This principle will surely lead man to Hell. It takes considerable discipline, prayer and faith to keep on the small "complicated" path to get to heaven.

This verse explains the relative number of those saved as opposed to those who are not. Salvation is surely attainable, but it requires work from those who truly want it.

Man wants to take the easy way through life, but the Christian will accept sacrifice of earthly pleasures for the rewards in heaven that await him.

*DAY 6*
*SUGGESTED READING*
*MATTHEW 16:25*

> **²⁵ For whosoever will save his life shall lose it: and whosoever will lose his life for my sake shall find it. (KJV)**

God allows us free will. Throughout the Bible he presents us with options on which path to take. For those who do not read Bible, they are subject to the will of Satan and forsake Christ. The will have the respect of fellow man but will ultimately lose his eternal life. This is a sure way to incur the wrath of God.

Choosing to sacrifice one's life for Christ, guarantees eternally life. This is not an easy thing to do. It requires self-sacrifice. God does not force this on us, he allows us to consider the options and make a choice.

To me, the choice is clear: death and eternal damnation or salvation and eternal life.

DAY 7
SUGGESTED READING
1 PETER 1:8 - 9

> **⁸ You love him, although you have not seen him, and you believe in him, although you do not now see him. So you rejoice with a great and glorious joy which words cannot express,**
>
> **⁹ because you are receiving the salvation of your souls, which is the purpose of your faith in him. (GNT)**

Blessed are those who had the opportunity to see and spend time with Jesus. To listen to his sermons, to see his miracles, to be in his presence would have been life altering.

Paul is teaching us that it is not necessary to see Christ to take advantage of his gifts. Sight is temporal and pertains to our Earthly life. Seeing with our spiritual eye is eternal.

These verses explain the modern Christian:

- Christians love Christ
- Christians believe in Christ
- Christians rejoice in Christ
- Christians are saved through Christ
- No Christian today has seen Christ

# WEEK 5
# SIN

DAY 1
SUGGESTED READING
ROMANS 3:23, GENESIS 3:1 - 7

## <sup>23</sup> For all have sinned, and come short of the glory of God (KJV)

When most people think of sin, they think of what they have done recently or even today. People deal with their sins after assigning levels to it. People tend to ignore those sins that they determine to be victimless.

Sin is a much deeper and older than this. Sin is any act contrary to the nature of God. It is a force of evil that originates from Satan. Sin began with Eve in Genesis.

Genesis 3:6-7

## <sup>6</sup> When the woman saw that the fruit of the tree was good for food and pleasing to the eye, and also desirable for gaining wisdom, she took some and ate it. She also gave some to her husband, who was with her, and he ate it.

## <sup>7</sup> Then the eyes of both of them were opened, and they realized they were naked; so they sewed fig leaves together and made coverings for themselves. (NIV)

This original sin is a concept of sinfulness where every human being is thereby affected. This is passed down from generation to generation and is the general character of all man.

*DAY 2*
*SUGGESTED READING*
*ROMANS 5:12*

**¹² Sin came into the world through one man, and his sin brought death with it. As a result, death has spread to the whole human race because everyone has sinned. (GNT)**

Paul confirms the concept of original sin. It explains man's condition of ungodliness.

I agree with the interpretation of Dr. Taylor; "The consequences of Christ's obedience extend as far as the consequences of Adam's disobedience. The consequences of Adam's disobedience extend to all mankind; and therefore, so do the consequences of Christ's obedience".

This is another example of the "Yin/Yang" of the Bible.

DAY 3
SUGGESTED READING
MARK 7:20 – 23

**[20] And he said, That which cometh out of the man, that defileth the man.**

**[21] For from within, out of the heart of men, proceed evil thoughts, adulteries, fornications, murders,**

**[22] Thefts, covetousness, wickedness, deceit, lasciviousness, an evil eye, blasphemy, pride, foolishness:**

**[23] All these evil things come from within and defile the man. (KJV)**

Jesus teaches that evil ideas will lead us to do immoral things. We need to guard our thoughts and our heart to stay righteous. Lack of God in our life leads to poor moral judgement and lack of ethical values.

If you look closely at these verses you will recognize that they are a restatement of the 10 Commandments. These laws are as pertinent in the Old Testament as they are in the New Testament.

*DAY 4*
*SUGGESTED READING*
*JOHN 8:34*

**³⁴ Jesus answered them, Verily, verily, I say unto you, Whosoever committeth sin is the servant of sin. (KJV)**

Consider the people who constantly and repeatedly commit Sin. They are servants of Sin. Satan has become their master. Sin is addictive. Once given to it, sin becomes easier and easier to do, with no regard to law but only satisfying lust. It falsely satisfies passions and desires. This is why it requires constant reinforcement.

The servant of Sin knows that they are headed down the path of eternal damnation. They feel that they cannot control their destiny.

The Christian needs to help those that want to change their ways with the message of sin forgiveness and salvation through Christ. Romans 3:23 – 24

DAY 5
SUGGESTED READING
PROVERBS 14:12

**$^{12}$ There is a way that appears to be right, but in the end it leads to death. (NIV)**

This letter to the Colossians came at the right time. Paul had learned that there were false teachers amongst them who insisted that certain spiritual rulers and authorities must be worshiped. The teachings were of pagan origin. Paul opposes these teachings and makes it clear that the gospel of Christ should be followed.

There are things that appear right and may even have some positive benefit, but in the end, they will be wolves in sheep's clothing. There could be courses of action that are even lawful in the eyes of man that lead to death.

Examine all things with the Laws of the Lord in mind. This is the gold standard and will keep one clear of deception.

*DAY 6*
*SUGGESTED READING*
*EZEKIEL 18:30*

**³⁰ Therefore I will judge you, O house of Israel, every one according to his ways, saith the Lord God. Repent, and turn yourselves from all your transgressions; so iniquity shall not be your ruin. (KJV)**

God does not want sinners to perish. He wants them to use their free will to accept him. God will deal with every one of us according to our own attitude towards Him.

In Ezekiel's dream, God tells him that repentance is the only way to salvation. He is speaking of everyone, not only the Jews as the scriptures state. Sin will keep us from God's salvation. This message is a fore bearer to the message of Christ and the disciples of Christ.

DAY 7
SUGGESTED READING
DANIEL 9:5

**⁵ We have sinned, and have committed iniquity, and have done wickedly, and have rebelled, even by departing from thy precepts and from thy judgments (KJV)**

Multiple notable interpretations of this verse suggest that there is a progression of sin. Four sins are being committed here. They are sins of deeds, sins of word, sins of thought and sins of apostasy. These sins correspond to the words: sin, iniquity, wickedly and rebelled. Daniel knows he is not without sin and includes himself with his people.

In comparison, Nehemiah also confesses his sins in a similar manner. He confesses errors in ignorance, sins by infirmity, habitually and willfully done wickedness and openly and obstinately rebelled against God.

We too, have sinned in manners according to the way of Man. We have departed from God's Law at some point. Do not forget this.

# WEEK 6
# ASSURANCE

DAY 1
SUGGESTED READING
PHILIPPIANS 4:6-7

> **⁶ Do not be anxious about anything, but in every situation, by prayer and petition, with thanksgiving, present your requests to God.**
>
> **⁷ And the peace of God, which transcends all understanding, will guard your hearts and your minds in Christ Jesus. (NIV)**

Everybody has anxiety in life. It is part of being human. Anxiety tends to start small and builds into a mountainous concern. However, there are times when anxiety starts to affect our lives. It presents as stress or fear. It can be disabling if allowed to build unchecked.

Many people seek medical attention for this disorder and get medication to counteract the effects of anxiety. Others will resort to other chemical means; alcohol, marijuana, etc.

The Christian has God. Through Jesus Christ, the troubles that are upsetting your peace can be given to God. He will take the burden and restore peace.

*DAY 2*
*SUGGESTED READING*
*PSALM 23:4*

**⁴ Yea, though I walk through the valley of the shadow of death, I will fear no evil: for thou art with me; thy rod and thy staff they comfort me. (KJV)**

Life is filled with perils. These are not always as dire as presented in this verse presented by David. Though our confidence is tested continuously.

When Life does get too trying, and we feel anxiety and fear, we have the Lord to fall back on. God promises to be there for us. He is our greatest protector and defender.

Do not be so afraid that you forget that God is there to help you through whatever assails you.

## DAY 3
## SUGGESTED READING
## PSALM 42:11

> **¹¹ Why, my soul, are you cast down?**
> **Why do you groan within me?**
> **Wait for God;**
> **I will yet thank Him,**
> **For He is my deliverance and my God. (MEV)**

God promises to be there for us. He cannot change this because God cannot lie.

Be patient, if you are sincere in your prayer, and it is in God's will, he will come to your assistance.

Always trust in the Lord. Present all your troubles to him. Don't be depressed or anxious. He is our refuge.

*DAY 4*
*SUGGESTED READING*
*ROMANS 8:39 39*

**nor height nor depth, nor anything else in all creation, will be able to separate us from the love of God in Christ Jesus our Lord. (KJV)**

If there is any doubt that Christians will always be bound to God, this verse removes it. Paul explains that there is nothing in the known universe that can separate us from God. Once we are bound to God, it is forever.

So fear not those that have been saved and departed from the path and wants to return. You have been saved. There is no need to be saved again. Repent your sins and strive to follow the path of righteousness. God remains there for you.

DAY 5
SUGGESTED READING
ISAIAH 43:2

**² When you pass through the waters,
I will be with you;
and when you pass through the rivers,
they will not sweep over you.
When you walk through the fire,
you will not be burned;
the flames will not set you ablaze. (NIV)**

Obviously, these literal problems are metaphors for figurative problems in our lives. No matter what our difficulties are, God is there to see us through. This is a testament of the good will of God.

Though these words were given to the people of Israel, Christians today can trust that he will be there to support and guide them.

*DAY 6*
*SUGGESTED READING*
*DUETERONOMY 31:8*

**⁸ The LORD himself goes before you and will be with you; he will never leave you nor forsake you. Do not be afraid; do not be discouraged. (NIV)**

Moses tells the people of Israel that Joshua will now lead them into the land promised by God. He also assures the people of Israel that God is with them. He may as well be speaking to us as Christians today.

God will never leave us. He is omnipresent and knows what we need and will assist us in accomplishing our goals. He will be there as a defender and will not let us be overwhelmed by our opponents.

Be strong in your faith and believe in the promises of God.

DAY 7
SUGGESTED READING
HEBREWS 6:11

> **[11] We desire that every one of you show the same diligence for the full assurance of hope to the end, (MEV)**

Hebrews teaches us that Jesus Christ is supreme in all things. We, in this world are in a sea of confusion and need an anchor. It is hard to keep focused on the Law of the Lord throughout life. Jesus is this anchor.

Staying diligent to the righteous life and having faith that the Lord will assure our hope is grounded in our level of belief. Continue to trust in the Lord at all times if you want to see your hopes realized.

Jesus says if we ask in his name it shall be given to us. Living the righteous life gives us the assurance that we need.

# WEEK 7
# THE BIBLE

DAY 1
SUGGESTED READING
2 TIMOTHY 3:16

**¹⁶ All scripture is given by inspiration of God, and is profitable for doctrine, for reproof, for correction, for instruction in righteousness (KJV)**

The Bible is the sacred writings of the Christian religion. It contains the Old Testament and the New Testament. It is written over, a period of 1500 years, by 40 authors.

The central message of the Bible is God's desire to have a personal relationship with each of us. He wants us to know him through His word and trust him emphatically.

The Bible answers the questions of righteous living. It also provides the details for attaining eternal life and the benefits thereof.

*DAY 2*
*SUGGESTED READING*
*2 PETER 1:20 - 21*

**²⁰ Knowing this first, that no prophecy of the scripture is of any private interpretation.**

**²¹ For the prophecy came not in old time by the will of man: but holy men of God spake as they were moved by the Holy Ghost. (KJV)**

Scripture was inspired by God. There were many religious persons who spoke prophecy from their god's, but the Bible was comprised of writings from holy men sanctified by God's spirit.

Scripture is the revelation of the mind of God. He inspired the holy men of the time through the Holy Spirit to speak and write his message. His intention is to have all man to seek its knowledge and understand the meaning behind the words.

Every Christians know by faith that the Bible is the word of God. It is our only scriptural source of knowledge. It is held in the highest esteem and reverence as it is the written word of God.

*DAY 3*
*SUGGESTED READING*
*JOHN 17:17*

## **¹⁷ Sanctify them through thy truth: thy word is truth. (KJV)**

We know that God's Word is truth. Jesus confirms this in this verse. Jesus is giving us his testimony that everything in the Bible is there by God's will and it is truth.

It is for the Christian to put those words into practice to be sanctified. We become empowered by His Spirit because of our faith and use these words to preach to others.

*DAY 4*
*SUGGESTED READING*
*PSALM 12:6*

> **⁶ The words of the LORD are pure words: as silver tried in a furnace of earth, purified seven times. (KJV)**

The word of God can be trusted as truth. They are holy words and not contaminated by man. These words are incorruptible.

Because they are pure, the words of the Bible can be trusted. They are generational and never expire or go out of style.

The word of God inspires Christians to be righteous. They strengthen the faith and moves the spirit within.

DAY 5
SUGGESTED READING
JOSHUA 1:8

**⁸ This book of the law shall not depart out of thy mouth; but thou shalt meditate therein day and night, that thou mayest observe to do according to all that is written therein: for then thou shalt make thy way prosperous, and then thou shalt have good success. (KJV)**

The Lord speaks to Joshua and charges him to follow the words of the Book of the Law. As the new leader of the people of Israel, all his judgements and rulings must be in accordance to the Law of the Lord.

Like Joshua, we must contemplate the Word of God day and night. The more we read and meditate, the more we will understand the blessings of the Lord.

*DAY 6*
*SUGGESTED READING*
*PSALM 119:89*

**⁸⁹ For ever, O Lord, thy word is settled in heaven. (KJV)**

God's word is eternal. The word was conceived by God and was in God's mind before the world was created and will be in place until the end of this time.

DAY 7
SUGGESTED READING
REVELATION 22:18

**[18] I testify to everyone who hears the words of the prophecy of this book: If anyone adds to these things, God shall add to him the plagues that are written in this book.**

**[19] And if anyone takes away from the words of the book of this prophecy, God shall take away his part out of the Book of Life and out of the Holy City and out of the things which are written in this book. (MEV)**

These are the words of God. They were written by holy men inspired by the Holy Spirit. If any words are changed, it is no longer the sanctified word of God.

The most common bible used today is the King James Version of 1611. There have been 4 revisions since that time that did not change the message in the text. These changes involved proofreading (what I call typos), printing or type (font), and orthographic (spelling). In addition, there have been a number of changes of punctuation and case.

Utmost care has been taken in any revision to the Bible. The warnings are clear. God does not want anyone to detract or add to His written Word

# WEEK 8
# BLESSED

DAY 1
SUGGESTED READING
NUMBERS 6:24 - 26

> [24] **The LORD bless thee, and keep thee:**
>
> [25] **The LORD make his face shine upon thee, and be gracious unto thee:**
>
> [26] **The LORD lift up his countenance upon thee, and give thee peace. (KJV)**

This benediction is commonly used at the beginning and end of life. It is frequently used to conclude worship services at church.

Originally, this blessing was given to the people of Israel in preparation for leaving Mount Sinai to continue to the promised land. The intention was to use this blessing daily as a reminder of the love of God.

Though this is a blessing for a journey, it applies to todays Christian. Remember the Lord is always with you. Take joy in this blessing.

DAY 2
SUGGESTED READING
PROVERBS 16:20

**[20] Whoever gives heed to instruction prospers,
and blessed is the one who trusts in the LORD.
(NIV)**

Anyone who manages his business and life sensibly and cautiously will most likely succeed in both. However, the one who seeks God's guidance in these affairs of life is blessed with greater happiness.

Trust in the Lord at all times. He will always be there to assist you in every aspect of your life.

DAY 3
SUGGESTED READING
MATTHEW 5:3 – 12

³ Blessed are the poor in spirit: for theirs is the kingdom of heaven.

⁴ Blessed are they that mourn: for they shall be comforted.

⁵ Blessed are the meek: for they shall inherit the earth.

⁶ Blessed are they which do hunger and thirst after righteousness: for they shall be filled.

⁷ Blessed are the merciful: for they shall obtain mercy.

⁸ Blessed are the pure in heart: for they shall see God.

⁹ Blessed are the peacemakers: for they shall be called the children of God.

¹⁰ Blessed are they which are persecuted for righteousness' sake: for theirs is the kingdom of heaven.

¹¹ Blessed are ye, when men shall revile you, and persecute you, and shall say all manner of evil against you falsely, for my sake.

**¹² Rejoice and be exceeding glad: for great is your reward in heaven: for so persecuted they the prophets which were before you. (KJV)**

Being blessed is to be sanctified or "made separate" in the eyes of God. One who incorporates these qualities of the Beautitudes into their lives becomes a member of a special blessed group. The Beautitudes have been regarded as timeless rules for righteous living

Jesus displayed all the qualities of the Beautitudes in his life on Earth. The Christian should strive to emulate these qualities as we strive to be like Christ. The Lord promises his blessings on you if you do.

DAY 4
SUGGESTED READING
PSALM 1:1

**1 Blessed is the man that walketh not in the counsel of the wicked,
Nor standeth in the way of sinners,
Nor sitteth in the seat of scoffers (ASV)**

Psalms begins with a contrast of the good man and the sinful man. The good man David refers to is the saved man. The blessed man has no appearance of evil in his life.

As you walk through life, avoid that which steers you away from the Laws of the Lord. Take pleasure in knowing that you are blessed for your perseverance.

*DAY 5*
*SUGGESTED READING*
*2 CORINTHIANS 9:8*

**⁸ And God is able to bless you abundantly, so that in all things at all times, having all that you need, you will abound in every good work. (NIV)**

We have heard the saying, "you get what you give". This principle implies that giving liberally will reward you in the end.

Paul implores the Corinthians to give generously. "Good will come to him who is generous and lends freely". (Psalm 112:5 NIV)

If God has blessed, you with abundance don't be stingy in sharing. It is unlikely that you will be reduced to poverty by giving. The person who charitably gives receives a divine blessing from the Lord who will keep him from want.

More importantly is the fact that our faith gives us assurance that God knows our heart and will provide for our future.

DAY 6
SUGGESTED READING
PROVERB 10:6 - 7

> **⁶ Blessings crown the head of the righteous,
> but violence overwhelms the mouth of the wicked.**
>
> **⁷ The name of the righteous is used in blessings,
> but the name of the wicked will rot. (NIV)**

The righteous are righteous by faith. Everything they do, they give consideration to Christ. As Christ is the head of the righteous, all his followers are so blessed.

We must remember Christ. He is the one that we will never forget. But what of us? Do we want to be remembered? How do we want to be remembered?

Be righteous in our life and we will be remembered for our righteousness. It is a testament to our faith.

*DAY 7*
*SUGGESTED READING*
*LIKE 6:22*

**²² Blessed are you when people hate you,**
**when they exclude you and insult you**
**and reject your name as evil,**
**because of the Son of Man. (NIV)**

How many times have you been excluded from groups that previously excepted you as a result of your faith. Sinners, even your friends, tend to change when exposed to the presence of the Holy Spirit.

Never give up on those who reject the gospel of Christ. Though they may treat you differently, God blesses you for being his representative to the sinners of the world.

# WEEK 9
# JESUS

DAY 1
SUGGESTED READING
JOHN 1:9 - 14

⁹ **The true light that gives light to everyone was coming into the world.**

¹⁰ **He was in the world, and though the world was made through him, the world did not recognize him.**

¹¹ **He came to that which was his own, but his own did not receive him.**

¹² **Yet to all who did receive him, to those who believed in his name, he gave the right to become children of God—**

¹³ **children born not of natural descent, nor of human decision or a husband's will, but born of God.**

¹⁴ **The Word became flesh and made his dwelling among us. We have seen his glory, the glory of the one and only Son, who came from the Father, full of grace and truth. (NIV)**

Jesus was the Word of God in the form of flesh. When he came into the world he was not recognized as the savior. Even with all the prophecy of the Old Testament, the Pharisees and elders did not except Jesus.

As he walked amongst man and gave his message to all who would listen, he started to have followers. Most of the groundwork for his ministry was due to the work of John the Baptist. The ordinary and poor were the first to accept Jesus and they became saved.

DAY 2
SUGGESTED READING
COLOSIANS 2:9

## ⁹ For in Christ all the fullness of the Deity lives in bodily form, (NIV)

In this verse, Paul explains that Jesus is the embodiment of God. The importance of this is to establish that his divinity is paramount to the understanding of his gospel. Everyone before and after him are messengers of his word.

As such, Jesus had the authority to give the gift of life. As John said, he baptizes with water, but Jesus baptizes with the Holy Spirit. Through Jesus, man saw God.

DAY 3
SUGGESTED READING
JOHN 10:28

**²⁸ And I give unto them eternal life; and they shall never perish, neither shall any man pluck them out of my hand. (KJV)**

Isn't this a wonderful gift that has been given to those that have received Jesus. This is gift is forever, in this life and after.

Only Jesus has the authority and the power to offer eternal life. It is freely given by the grace of God.

*DAY 4*
*SUGGESTED READING*
*ACTS 4:12*

**¹² Salvation is to be found through him alone; in all the world there is no one else whom God has given who can save us. (GNT)**

God offered salvation, first to the Jews, then to the Gentiles. In order to be saved, one must believe in Christ and accept him as their personal savior.

This is the only way to salvation and eternal life. Jesus is the conduit between God and man. In this verse, Peter proclaimed Jesus as the Messiah.

Understand that there is no other way to be saved but through Jesus.

DAY 5
SUGGESTEDD READING
JOHN 1:1

**1 In the beginning was the Word, and the Word was with God, and the Word was God. (KJV)**

Jesus is identified at the beginning of the New Testament as part of the Holy Trinity. Here he is referenced as the Word of God. He is also identified as being with God and is, in fact, God.

Throughout the New Testament he can be identified with any of these terms. As for his physical being, he is presented as the son of God. In any case, Jesus commands the utmost respect, worship and devotion.

The implication of this verse is that Jesus was part of the creation of all things. So life itself is what Jesus brings to this world.

DAY 6
SUGGESTED READING
JOHN 8:12

**¹² Then spake Jesus again unto them, saying, I am the light of the world: he that followeth me shall not walk in darkness, but shall have the light of life. (KJV)**

Jesus is considered the spiritual light. This light prevails over darkness being the metaphor for sin. Those who have the light of Jesus to guide them will have confidence in any situation.

This verse is an acknowledgement by Jesus to the righteous who follow him. The righteous always seek the light.

*DAY 7*
*SUGGESTED READING*
*ISAIAH 9:6*

**⁶ For unto us a child is born, unto us a son is given: and the government shall be upon his shoulder: and his name shall be called Wonderful, Counsellor, The mighty God, The everlasting Father, The Prince of Peace. (KJV)**

Isaiah prophesizes about a time of peace. This time will be led by one who receives the kingdom of Earth from his Father in heaven.

He tells us that the child that will be delivered to man will not be of this world but from Heaven. It is understood that this child is the Messiah.

# WEEK 10
# CHILDREN

DAY 1
SUGGESTED READING
PROVERBS 22:6

**⁶ Train up a child in the way he should go: and when he is old, he will not depart from it. (KJV)**

A great duty of every parent is to raise their children in a way to be successful in this world. Children should be given instruction in the ways of man and the laws of man and society, that they make their way according to man's law.

More importantly though is instruction in the Laws of the Lord. Children should be trained regarding the Great Commandant and the Golden Rule. Early training and continued training will guard them against corruption and keep them humble. The Lord will reward them for their perseverance.

Children trained in the gospel have a better chance of maintaining their lives in the way of the Lord. They in turn will impart this to their children.

DAY 2
SUGGESTED READING
DEUTERONOMY 6:6 - 9

> **⁶ These commandments that I give you today are to be on your hearts.**
>
> **⁷ Impress them on your children. Talk about them when you sit at home and when you walk along the road, when you lie down and when you get up.**
>
> **⁸ Tie them as symbols on your hands and bind them on your foreheads.**
>
> **⁹ Write them on the doorframes of your houses and on your gates. (NIV)**

It is difficult to keep the attention of children for long. To teach your children about the Laws of the Lord, be patient and diligent. This is important work of the Lord.

Sit with your children and repeat the Laws of the Lord through scripture memory and through examples. Let them see how important this is to you and them.

Have reminders in your home to reinforce the importance of God. Children will follow the behaviors of their parents. God will be there to help you be good teachers.

DAY 3
SUGGESTED READING
DEUTERONOMY 4:9

**⁹ Only be careful and watch yourselves closely so that you do not forget the things your eyes have seen or let them fade from your heart as long as you live. Teach them to your children and to their children after them. (NIV)**

The road to be a good Christian is difficult. You have been taught many things about God and his Law. These are lessons that are hard learned and have involved a good portion of your life.

Never forget these lessons and teach them to your children and to your children's children. They will do the same to maintain the covenant of the Lord.

*DAY 4*
*SUGGESTED READING*
*PROVERBS 23:13 - 14*

**¹³ Do not withhold discipline from a child;
if you punish them with the rod, they will not die.**

**¹⁴ Punish them with the rod
and save them from death. (NIV)**

This can be difficult for the modern Christian. Our society frowns on corporal punishment. Child psychologist expound the dangers of violence physically or verbally to children.

God is not saying to destroy your child. Children will limit test at all stages of their lives. If they can get away with bad decisions and behaviors early, they will continue into their adult life. They will become servants of Satan.

Discipline with a good spanking early and pertinent to the infraction, with explanation of why they are being disciplined is the parent's way of encouraging good behavior and good decision making.

This will develop a respect for right thinking and behavior. The parent can save their child from the path of eternal death.

DAY 5
SUGGESTED READING
EPHESIANS 6:4

**⁴ Fathers, do not exasperate your children; instead, bring them up in the training and instruction of the Lord. (NIV)**

Children want to please their parents. Their obedience demonstrates their reverence. It has been said this is the duty of a child.

Then what is the duty of the parent? It is important for the parent to give the child instruction that is appropriate for their age and maturity.

This includes religious education also. The knowledge and duty to God should be imparted by every Christian parent with repetition and patience. If children are required to learn about God and his Laws, make it reasonable for them to learn and they will have success.

*DAY 6*
*SUGGESTED READING*
*HEBREWS 12:11*

**11 No discipline seems pleasant at the time, but painful. Later on, however, it produces a harvest of righteousness and peace for those who have been trained by it. (NIV)**

It is difficult to impose discipline on one's children. It is painful for all parties involved.

Discipline results in a structured life with understanding of right versus wrong. With early discipline behaviors are created that require less reason to discipline as the child gets older. This is part of their training and promotes maturity.

DAY 7
SUGGESTED READING
PROVERBS 17:6

**⁶ Children's children are a crown to the aged, and parents are the pride of their children. (NIV)**

Children that have been raised right in the eyes of the Lord are a major source of pride for their parents. It is a greater honor to see that their children are raising their children the same way.

The children will be proud of the parents in turn. This is a spiritually healthy family.

# WEEK 11
# CHRISTIAN LIVING

DAY 1
SUGGESTED READING
ROMANS 12:2

**² Do not conform yourselves to the standards of this world, but let God transform you inwardly by a complete change of your mind. Then you will be able to know the will of God—what is good and is pleasing to him and is perfect. (GNT)**

The Christian must remember that though we exist in the world of man, we must not act as other men. We are called to God to do his will.

Keeping the faith and studying his Word will transform you internally and progressively turns you into a higher mode of existence, in accordance with God's will.

*DAY 2*
*SUGGESTED READING*
*COLOSSIANS 3: 5 - 8*

**⁵ Put to death, therefore, whatever belongs to your earthly nature: sexual immorality, impurity, lust, evil desires and greed, which is idolatry.**

**⁶ Because of these, the wrath of God is coming.**

**⁷ You used to walk in these ways, in the life you once lived.**

**⁸ But now you must also rid yourselves of all such things as these: anger, rage, malice, slander, and filthy language from your lips. (NIV)**

Never forget we are Christians. We have chosen to life the life of Christ. We have given up all the sins of our past for they led to eternal death.

These verses remind us of the ways of man. All this sin keeps us from obeying God. It is a sad state in the world that people will accept this as the way to live.

DAY 3
SUGGESTED READING
EPHESIANS 4:32

**³² Be kind and compassionate to one another, forgiving each other, just as in Christ God forgave you. (NIV)**

Always be kind to everyone. Be kind in your heart and this will be projected unto others. It is not hard to be compassionate. It is how you would like people to treat you.

If you have been harmed, be quick to forgive. Jesus teaches us this in Our Lord's Prayer. Be genuine in your forgiveness then forget about the offense as God forgets when he forgives.

*DAY 4*
*SUGGESTED READING*
*ROMANS 12:1*

**¹² I beseech you therefore, brethren, by the mercies of God, that ye present your bodies a living sacrifice, holy, acceptable unto God, which is your reasonable service. (KJV)**

Christians present themselves in two ways. They present themselves to God in a righteous, spiritual way. Then they present themselves to man in a way that emulates the righteous, spiritual way.

God has given us his laws and ask that we be faithful and obey his laws. This is not an unreasonable request of a Christian.

DAY 5
SUGGESTED READING
JAMES 4:11 - 12

**¹¹ Speak not evil one of another, brethren. He that speaketh evil of his brother, and judgeth his brother, speaketh evil of the law, and judgeth the law: but if thou judge the law, thou art not a doer of the law, but a judge.**

**¹² There is one lawgiver, who is able to save and to destroy: who art thou that judgest another? (KJV)**

Christians must stay humble, to God and to his fellow man. We must not judge lest we be judged. Besides, we are not the judge. The Lord is the judge.

When we judge, we take a position of being better than the person we are judging. This presumption leads us down a dangerous path. Be careful not to open the door for sin to enter your life.

God is the judge. He can do this because he is the maker of the Laws. He can also do this because he is just. He is without fault. If one presumes they are the same, then they surely are fooling themselves.

*DAY 6*
*SUGGESTED READING*
*MATTHEW 6:24*

**²⁴ No man can serve two masters: for either he will hate the one and love the other; or else he will hold to the one and despise the other. Ye cannot serve God and mammon. (KJV)**

"Mammon", this is a metaphor for anything that is evil. In this case, it is money. It also represents any other earthly possession.

Man must choose between heavenly and earthly possessions. One cannot serve two masters. To be torn between allegiances causes resentment towards one or the other.

DAY 7
SUGGESTED READING
ROMANS 12:17 - 21

**¹⁷ Recompense to no man evil for evil. Provide things honest in the sight of all men.**

**¹⁸ If it be possible, as much as lieth in you, live peaceably with all men.**

**¹⁹ Dearly beloved, avenge not yourselves, but rather give place unto wrath: for it is written, Vengeance is mine; I will repay, saith the Lord.**

**²⁰ Therefore if thine enemy hunger, feed him; if he thirst, give him drink: for in so doing thou shalt heap coals of fire on his head.**

**²¹ Be not overcome of evil, but overcome evil with good. (KJV)**

We must always remain faithful to the teachings of Jesus. It is easy to slip and let emotions get control of our life. God will affect judgement according to one's deeds.

Keeping in God is the way, not only to righteous living, but also, to righteous thinking. As we become more spiritual, we will act according to his will and not the will of man.

# WEEK 12
# THE CHURCH

*DAY 1*
*SUGGESTED READING*
*EPHESIANS 2:19 - 22*

**[19] So then, you Gentiles are not foreigners or strangers any longer; you are now citizens together with God's people and members of the family of God.**

**[20] You, too, are built upon the foundation laid by the apostles and prophets, the cornerstone being Christ Jesus himself.**

**[21] He is the one who holds the whole building together and makes it grow into a sacred temple dedicated to the Lord.**

**[22] In union with him you too are being built together with all the others into a place where God lives through his Spirit. (GNT)**

Paul explains to the non-Jewish Ephesians in this letter the recipe for establishing their church. The most important message being delivered is that all should be included who has belief in the gospel of Christ.

Paul emphasizes that Gentile Christians are equal and should be treated as such. Anyone who excepts Christ as their savior is transformed spiritually and enjoys the eternal gifts given from God

*DAY 2*
*SUGGESTED READING*
*1 TIMOTHY 3:15*

**¹⁵ if I am delayed, you will know how people ought to conduct themselves in God's household, which is the church of the living God, the pillar and foundation of the truth. (NIV)**

The church of God is only God's household if it remains true. It is emphatic that the priest of the church are true men of God with the foundation being built with Jesus Christ as the cornerstone.

If the leaders of the church set the example, the members will follow suit. The priest are the stewards of God and will deliver the message of Jesus and Laws of the Lord. They reinforce the ways of righteousness and wholesome behavior.

God's household extends to the home also. The same conduct is expected by the head of the household.

DAY 3
SUGGESTED READING
1 CORINTHIANS 14:26

**²⁶ What then shall we say, brothers and sisters? When you come together, each of you has a hymn, or a word of instruction, a revelation, a tongue or an interpretation. Everything must be done so that the church may be built up. (NIV)**

The members of the church of Corinth all wanted to offer what gifts they had to the service. This was very unorganized, and the leadership of the church meetings were a rotating responsibility. This can work in a very close-knit congregation. However, it could also cause problems as members may want to monopolize the time or feel that their agenda was more important.

Though this is one way of doing things, Paul gave them a method that would work better for social worship. Paul's method is what most church leaders use today. "Let all things be done decently and in order." (1 CORINTHIANS 14:40) Paul wanted church meetings to benefit all the members of the congregation. He did not want to dampen the enthusiasm of the Holy Spirit.

DAY 4
SUGGESTED READING
1 CORINTHIANS 12:12 - 14

**¹² For as the body is one, and hath many members, and all the members of that one body, being many, are one body: so also is Christ.**

**¹³ For by one Spirit are we all baptized into one body, whether we be Jews or Gentiles, whether we be bond or free; and have been all made to drink into one Spirit.**

**¹⁴ For the body is not one member, but many. (KJV)**

Christ is the head of his church. Christians are the body of his church. They become part of the whole through baptism. This outward display of devotion represents the rebirth of one's soul to one of eternal salvation. This is available to all who seek redemption.

As members of one body, all Christians have a mutual dependence unto each other in the church. None are saved to be isolated but are to be joined as a group with many people of all nations.

DAY 5
SUGGESTED READING
1 CORINTHIANS 3:17

> **¹⁷ If any man defile the temple of God, him shall God destroy; for the temple of God is holy, which temple ye are. (KJV)**

It is accepted everywhere that the Church is a holy place. Gentiles and non-Gentiles alike are of this opinion. Regardless of what man law will do to those who defile the church, God commanded death.

God views the Church as sacred and inviolable. This building is holy as his presence dwells there. Aside from physical assaults on the church, there is also spiritual assault. Corrupt teaching will make the church unholy. This leads its members into a spiritually dangerous place. God will not leave the leaders of these churches unpunished.

The verse extends holiness to the individual also. As Christians, we are commanded to respect our bodies and souls with the same reverence we would the church.

DAY 6
SUGGESTED READING
MATTHEW 16:18

**¹⁸ And I say also unto thee, That thou art Peter, and upon this rock I will build my church; and the gates of hell shall not prevail against it. (KJV)**

Jesus set Peter apart from the other disciples by designating him the "rock I will build my church; and the gates of hell shall not prevail against it" (KJV). Jesus must have felt that his faith and trust was unparalleled.

Instilling the gospel of Christ properly to the people is the spiritual church for the physical church to follow. Correct training is the foundation.

*DAY 7*
*SUGGESTED READING*
*HEBREWS 10:25*

**²⁵ not giving up meeting together, as some are in the habit of doing, but encouraging one another—and all the more as you see the Day approaching. (NIV)**

It is a sacred duty for Christians to meet together. In doing so they enhance their spirituality. Group meetings allow Christians to share and grow together.

Christians should also meet with non-Christians. If the Christian can understand their position, they may be able to open the door for them.

Keep in mind that the Day of the Lord is coming. Fellowship could not be more important than it is now with all the signs and prophecies appear to be presenting themselves.

# WEEK 13
# COMFORT

*DAY 1*
*SUGGESTED READING*
*PSALM 55:22*

**²² Leave your troubles with the LORD,
and he will defend you;
he never lets honest people be defeated. (GNT)**

God does not want to see us suffering. He would rather see us happy.

God not only wants us to bring our problems to him, he is willing take on the burden. It does not matter the size of the problem or how often we pray to him about it.

We must believe and trust in God with all our heart. We must pray in earnest to him. If it fits into God's plan, he will answer our prayers.

Remember, though the answer may not be exactly what we want, God will always do what is best for us.

DAY 2
SUGGESTED READING
1 PETER 5:6-7

> **⁶ Humble yourselves therefore under the mighty hand of God, that he may exalt you in due time:**
>
> **⁷ Casting all your care upon him; for he careth for you. (KJV)**

It is difficult for one to be humble. This is more difficult as one gets more successful in life. Very successful people tend to have greater problems than those that are humble in their modicum of success.

The problem with the very successful is that they trust in themselves to solve all the problems of their life. They rarely rely on God to help them.

The solution to all problems in life, whether very successful or mildly successful or not successful at all, is complete, total trust in the Lord. Any problem; business, family, personal, financial, the future, faith, can be solved with reliance on the Lord.

God want us to bring all our problems to him. He wants us to live in joy and comfort. God is listening.

DAY 3
SUGGESTED READING
JEREMIAH 29:11

**¹¹ For I know the plans I have for you," declares the LORD, "plans to prosper you and not to harm you, plans to give you hope and a future. (NIV)**

This is a promise. God is assuring us a good future. He is not asking for us to do something for him but upon his mercies he provides for us.

The beauty of this promise is in the fact that it cannot change. God has stated this, so it is fact. Unchangeable then and now or it would mean God can change his mind. We know that this cannot happen.

That being said, this is an expectation. Have no doubt that this is the plan for us as Christians.

*DAY 4*
*SUGGESTED READING*
*NAHUM 1:7*

**⁷ The LORD is good,**
**a refuge in times of trouble.**
**He cares for those who trust in him, (NIV)**

This is a prophecy to the people who believes in the Lord by his prophet Nahum. At the time it was for the Jews. But it applies to the modern-day Christian.

Its message is clear. If one has trouble the Lord will watch over them that believes and trust in him.

DAY 5
SUGGESTED READING
2 CORINTHIANS 1:3 - 4

**³ Praise be to the God and Father of our Lord Jesus Christ, the Father of compassion and the God of all comfort,**

**⁴ who comforts us in all our troubles, so that we can comfort those in any trouble with the comfort we ourselves receive from God. (NIV)**

This message from Paul reminds the believers in Corinth that the Lord will always be there to provide comfort to the soul. Paul knows this from experience.

The comfort gained from the Lord can also be imparted to others who are troubled. It is a great opportunity for the Christian to bear their testimony of how God will come to the aid of those who are having difficulty in their life.

*DAY 6*
*SUGGESTED READING*
*MATTHEW 11:28 – 30*

**²⁸ "Come to me, all you who are weary and burdened, and I will give you rest.**

**²⁹ Take my yoke upon you and learn from me, for I am gentle and humble in heart, and you will find rest for your souls.**

**³⁰ For my yoke is easy and my burden is light."
(NIV)**

Metaphorically, one can look at this verse and realize that Jesus is saying believe in me, learn from me and then follow me. In this way, one's life becomes less complicated and troubled. One's burden is now lightened with Christ directing it.

Another way to interpret these verses is to contemplate the ministry of the Christian. It is difficult and involves all persons in this world. Non-believers do not want to give up their earthly possessions or ideologies to live a life of humility.

As frustrating as it can be for the Christian, faith in the Lord will lighten the load. This reassurance of relief provides comfort and keeps the faithful motivated.

DAY 7
SUGGESTED READING
ISAIAH 41:10

**¹⁰ So do not fear, for I am with you;
do not be dismayed, for I am your God.
I will strengthen you and help you;
I will uphold you with my righteous right hand.
(NIV)**

Satan knows that he can shake our faith if we are afraid. The Lord knows this too. He tells us not to fear for he is with us.

We should take comfort in this fact and rely on it when fear creeps into the periphery of our minds. The Lord wants us to know that he will not abandon us when we are troubled or afraid. Jesus Himself said, " Teaching them to observe all things whatsoever I have commanded you: and, lo, I am with you always, even unto the end of the world." (Matthew 28:20 KJV) Christians have nothing to fear nor anyone to fear.

# WEEK 14
# DEATH

DAY 1
SUGGESTED READING
JOHN 11:25 - 26

**²⁵ Jesus said unto her, I am the resurrection, and the life: he that believeth in me, though he were dead, yet shall he live:**

**²⁶ And whosoever liveth and believeth in me shall never die. Believest thou this? (KJV)**

Jesus promises resurrection and life after physical death. Yes, death will happen to us all, but this does not kill our spiritual self. Jesus takes possession of resurrection and states emphatically that he is the resurrection and the life.

Believe in Jesus. God will only grant eternal life in proportion to their belief in Jesus. When Martha received Jesus into her home and her brother had died from sickness, she had no doubt that he would be resurrected. She just did not expect it to be immediately.

Jesus was true to his promise and resurrected her brother on the spot, thus proving that death had no ultimate power over him.

*DAY 2*
*SUGGESTED READING*
*ROMANS 6:23*

**²³ For the wages of sin is death; but the gift of God is eternal life through Jesus Christ our Lord. (KJV)**

Wages have always been given for work that has been done. It is not typically paid in advance but honored at the completion of the job. In this way the wages are earned. This verse presents Sin as the employer of the work to be done. Sin is bound by law to pay the wages.

I once read a commentary to this verse that said, "A man may merit hell, but he cannot merit heaven." How true is this I thought? We deserve hell because of our sin, but the free gift of God is eternal life through the belief and acceptance of his son Jesus Christ.

Be always thankful that God, in his gracious love for us, has provided a way for the righteous to be saved.

*DAY 3*
*SUGGESTED READING*
*JOB1:21*

**²¹ And said, Naked came I out of my mother's womb, and naked shall I return thither: the LORD gave, and the LORD hath taken away; blessed be the name of the LORD. (KJV)**

Job understood a concept that all Christians understand. Life is given to us as a free gift of God. We had no part of the conception of our life. We did nothing to earn the right to live. We have no idea when our life will end.

Be thankful for the opportunity to live. Make the best of the time that God has given you. Honor the Lord with your life for there is no other that has the power to give this gift.

*DAY 4*
*SUGGESTED READING*
*PSALM 116:15*

## **¹⁵ Precious in the sight of the LORD is the death of his saints. (KJV)**

The Lord is very aware of the death of his saints. He cares because these are people who have given their lives to him. The saints preach the Word of God, spread the gospel of Jesus and live according to his Laws. They are an example of pious living.

We are the Saints. Be aware of that daily and pray to live up to the standard every. The Lord is there with you and will give you the support that you need.

Don't fear death for the Lord is there looking over you. This is his promise. Remember that the death of a saint is the relief of the difficult trials and efforts of this earthly life to the restful peace of eternal life. God sees the death of his children as a restful state that is precious to Him.

*DAY 5*
*SUGGESTED READING*
*ROMANS 14:8*

**⁸ If we live, we live for the Lord; and if we die, we die for the Lord. So, whether we live or die, we belong to the Lord. (NIV)**

The purpose of Christian life is to promote the gospel of Christ. In life, we do these things willingly and with love as required by the Lord. The Christian life separates us from that of the non-believer.

In death, we still belong to Christ. Though our physical body is in the grave, our soul continues to exist in the ethereal plane and belongs to the Lord. Remember, the Lord is master of both the living and the dead.

*DAY 6*
*SUGGESTED READING*
*EZEKIEL 18:32*

**[32] For I take no pleasure in the death of anyone, declares the Sovereign LORD. Repent and live! (NIV)**

As Christians we know the truths; "All have sinned" and "the wages of sin is death". God takes displeasure in sin; therefore, he takes displeasure in the resultant death.

God provides an alternative to death. Repentance. God tells us what we need to do to live. He provides his son to take away the sins of man so if one repents, ask for forgiveness and accepts Christ he will live.

DAY 7
SUGGESTED READING
ECCLESIASTES 3:1 - 2

**¹ There is a time for everything,
and a season for every activity under the heavens:**

**² a time to be born and a time to die,
a time to plant and a time to uproot, (NIV)**

All things have a beginning and an end. Such also is the case for man. Since no one knows when they are to die, there is nothing one can do to prevent or extend it.

Use the time the Lord has given you to be the best Christian you can be. Praise the Lord everyday and in all circumstances. Spread the gospel of Christ. In the end you will be remembered by both man and God.

# WEEK 15
# DISOBEDIENCE

DAY 1
SUGGESTED READING
DEUTERONOMY 28:15

**¹⁵ However, if you do not obey the LORD your God and do not carefully follow all his commands and decrees I am giving you today, all these curses will come on you and overtake you: (NIV)**

The first 14 verses of Deuteronomy discuss the blessings of the Lord to his people. Starting from the 15th verse, the Lord gives his curse.

The Lord states that if we do not keep his commandments we will not enjoy his blessings but will endure his curse. This curse stays with us and follows us wherever we go. It disrupts our peace and takes away from any enjoyment of life. Guilt will be ever present in our life.

DAY 2
SUGGESTED READING
1 SAMUEL 12:15

**¹⁵ But if you do not obey the L**ORD**, and if you rebel against his commands, his hand will be against you, as it was against your ancestors. (NIV)**

The Lord does not tolerate disobedience now or ever. He could not have behaved in any other way. If so, he would be inconsistent. That would disrupt his sovereignty and make Him less than perfect. In a situation like that, the whole of the Bible fails.

But this is not the case. God will punish you as he has always punished. He will punish in the same way as always. None can hide or escape God's judgement. Thus, God is consistent.

DAY 3
SUGGESTED READING
JAMES 1:14 - 15

> **¹⁴ But we are tempted when we are drawn away and trapped by our own evil desires.**
>
> **¹⁵ Then our evil desires conceive and give birth to sin; and sin, when it is full-grown, gives birth to death. (GNT)**

The Buddhist have a belief in a philosophy called The Noble Truths. One of these truths states that suffering comes from desire. Desire is the root of all suffering and is also the root of all Sin. It is not surprising that the ancient Buddhist saw desire as the ultimate problem for man.

We are always tempted to Sin in the same way. It starts as something desirable either for profit or pleasure. How we get corrupted is in the ease of which it is to satisfy the desire. Giving into the desire mentally or physically is the finality of the Sin.

Never think that temptation is a method God uses to test our faith. It is always a tool of Satan. The temptation is not the sin. It is giving into the temptation and turning from the righteous path that makes it a Sin. God will never tempt man to do evil. He would never challenge man to disobey his Laws.

*DAY 4*
*SUGGESTED READING*
*REVELATIONS 21:8*

**⁸ But the cowardly, the unbelieving, the vile, the murderers, the sexually immoral, those who practice magic arts, the idolaters and all liars— they will be consigned to the fiery lake of burning sulfur. This is the second death." (NIV)**

Many are those that will suffer the second death. All will die once and then all will be resurrected again at the appointed time for judgement. The terror of the first death pales in comparison to the second death.

The identity of those not headed towards heaven is made easy for the Christian to see so that they can help guide these transgressors toward God.

*DAY 5*
*SUGGESTED READING*
*1 JOHN 3:6 – 10*

> **⁶ So if we stay close to him, obedient to him, we won't be sinning either; but as for those who keep on sinning, they should realize this: They sin because they have never really known him or become his.**
>
> **⁷ Oh, dear children, don't let anyone deceive you about this: if you are constantly doing what is good, it is because you are good, even as he is.**
>
> **⁸ But if you keep on sinning, it shows that you belong to Satan, who since he first began to sin has kept steadily at it. But the Son of God came to destroy these works of the devil.**
>
> **⁹ The person who has been born into God's family does not make a practice of sinning because now God's life is in him; so he can't keep on sinning, for this new life has been born into him and controls him—he has been *born again*.**
>
> **¹⁰ So now we can tell who is a child of God, and who belongs to Satan. Whoever is living a life of sin and doesn't love his brother shows that he is not in God's family; (TLB)**

John describes the dichotomy between the Christian and the non-believer. The Christian, due to the nature of their duty to God is biased not to sin. This spiritual principle keeps them from entertaining sinful behavior. The non-believer, on the other hand, typically neglect spiritual things. Even those that profess to believe in God, this is more for preservation of their image to man, will not abide in His laws or except Christ as their savior. The non-believer will frequently have disdain and hate for Christians, where Christians have love and pity for non-believers.

DAY 6
SUGGESTED READING
JAMES 2:10

**¹⁰ If someone obeys all of God's laws except one, that person is guilty of breaking all of them. (GW)**

Though this appears to be very unforgiving it is logical when considering the nature of God. God is without sin and this would go against his nature to allow even 1 transgression to get into heaven.

It has been accomplished though. Jesus is the personification of God's Law and never broke one of them. But Jesus is the essence of God in human form. He also is without sin by nature.

We cannot be that perfect but through Jesus we can be forgiven for the Sins that we commit. This is the authority given to Jesus from God.

DAY 7
SUGGESTED READING
HEBREWS 10:26 - 31

**26 If we deliberately keep on sinning after we have received the knowledge of the truth, no sacrifice for sins is left,**

**27 but only a fearful expectation of judgment and of raging fire that will consume the enemies of God.**

**28 Anyone who rejected the law of Moses died without mercy on the testimony of two or three witnesses.**

**29 How much more severely do you think someone deserves to be punished who has trampled the Son of God underfoot, who has treated as an unholy thing the blood of the covenant that sanctified them, and who has insulted the Spirit of grace?**

**30 For we know him who said, "It is mine to avenge; I will repay," and again, "The Lord will judge his people."**

**31 It is a dreadful thing to fall into the hands of the living God. (NIV)**

This is a warning to us as Christians. We must always remember our duty to the Lord who has saved us from eternal damnation. God is slow to anger but his judgement is terrible.

For me, it is difficult to imagine the Christian that has willingly rejected the protection and guidance of the Lord. I can't imagine a circumstance that they could not ask God for help.

We can only try and help this person return to God. We must help this person with love and not judge them. We do not know what led them to their current situation.

# WEEK 16
# DOUBT

DAY 1
SUGGESTED READING
JAMES 1:6

**⁶ But when you ask, you must believe and not doubt, because the one who doubts is like a wave of the sea, blown and tossed by the wind. (NIV)**

Doubt is the wavering between belief and unbelief with leaning towards the unbelief. Doubt is a result of a weakness in faith. It is in times of trial that we have our faith tested.

Faith is the operating principle for Christian life. It is the reliance on the character of God and the promises that he has made to us. God is always ready to answer prayer however, without faith there is no chance that this will happen.

We must pray to God with resolute confidence and trust that God will do what is in his will and best for us.

*DAY 2*
*SUGGESTED READING*
*ROMANS 14:23*

**²³ But whoever has doubts is condemned if they eat, because their eating is not from faith; and everything that does not come from faith is sin. (NIV)**

We have all heard the saying, "if you have doubt, don't do it". That is the message here. If you can't do something without full conviction that what your doing is right, there is sin involved.

This verse has universal application. This is not to say that every doubtful act is sinful. The act may be acceptable to non-Christians, but the Christian should not put their soul at risk. The Christian sins if they perform an act that they think is wrong. It is not worth worrying over after the act is performed.

*DAY 3*
*SUGGESTED READING*
*MATTHEW 28:17*

**¹⁷ When they saw him, they worshiped him; but some doubted. (NIV)**

Seeing Jesus after they saw him die was difficult for some to understand. This went against everything in their experience. We too are exposed to situations that, in spite of evidence, have a hard time believing.

It's a matter of faith. Jesus expects us to believe in him whether he is there or not. We must believe all that has been given to us through his Word is true.

*DAY 4*
*SUGGESTED READING*
*MARK 4:40*

**⁴⁰ He said to his disciples, "Why are you so afraid? Do you still have no faith?" (NIV)**

Jesus rebukes his disciples after he saves them from a storm at sea. His disciples are somewhat worried that the storm would consume him, but they had seen the works of Jesus and knew that since he was there, he would save them.

Fear and doubt is part of our earthly experience. If we let them, they will consume us. We should never question our faith. We must trust in the Lord at all times and with all our heart. Jesus is always with us spiritually to see us through these trying times.

*DAY 5*
*SUGGESTED READING*
*LUKE 24:11*

## **¹¹ And their words seemed to them as idle tales, and they believed them not. (KJV)**

The disciples did not believe it when they were told of the resurrection of Jesus. This is amazing since Jesus had prepared them in advance for this. How could they have forgotten what he had told them?

This seems to occur in the modern world when sharing the gospel of Christ to the non-believer world. Take heart and don't lose faith. Continue sharing with love and compassion and the Lord will help them understand.

*DAY 6*
*SUGGESTED READING*
*LUKE 24:37 - 38*

**[37] They were terrified, thinking that they were seeing a ghost. [38] But he said to them, "Why are you alarmed? Why are these doubts coming up in your minds? (GNT)**

This reaction to seeing Jesus resurrected is not surprising. His disciples had last seen him crucified. But had Jesus not prepared them for this? On multiple occasions he spoke to them about his resurrection.

Christians today are as prepared as the disciples had been. We are told over and over that Jesus will return. We long for it. Be ready when he does come. Don't be alarmed!

*DAY 7*
*SUGGESTED READING*
*MATTHEW 14:31*

**³¹ Immediately Jesus reached out his hand and caught him. "You of little faith," he said, "why did you doubt?" (NIV)**

Never weaken in your faith. Doubt will always be part of our life and we should know that Jesus is there to get us through our struggle.

If there is a cause for doubt in your life, pray to God. He will hear you and come to your aide. Never doubt this. He tells us to bring our troubles to him. He is our refuge.

# WEEK 17
# GIVING

*DAY 1*
*SUGGESTED READING*
*DEURERONOMY 15:10*

**¹⁰ Give generously to them and do so without a grudging heart; then because of this the LORD your God will bless you in all your work and in everything you put your hand to. (NIV)**

To the poor and needy, give what you can. Donate usable items to Good Will or the Salvation Army. Keep the less fortunate in your mind and heart.

It makes my heart saddened to see these people. I always donate and give when I can. I don't do this because I am supposed to, but because I want to.

Though the Lord promises to reward generous giving, this is never the motivation behind a giving heart.

*DAY 2*
*SUGGESTED READING*
*DEUTERONOMY 16:17*

**¹⁷ Every man shall give as he is able, according to the blessing of the L**ORD **thy God which he hath given thee. (KJV)**

We as being blessed by God need remember where we came from. We must remember that the gifts we are given is through our faith in Jesus Christ who gave his life that we are saved.

This salvation has transformed us and places us into a selected group that is looked over by God. This grace has made us fortunate in life.

Do not forget to share what we can to assist others less fortunate. Show them God's love through your actions. Share your testimony with them. Let them understand that through God there is salvation, not only for earthly things but also for the soul.

DAY 3
SUGGESTED READING
PROVERBS 28:27

**²⁷ Those who give to the poor will lack nothing, but those who close their eyes to them receive many curses. (NIV)**

If you give to the poor you will be blessed. Even if you only have little, God will not let you become impoverished. The affluent will argue the opposite and God will remember this also.

Try when you can to help those that you see in need of basic necessities. Don't turn a blind eye to them. Regardless of how they got in their situation, that is not for us to judge. Have a compassionate heart and try to help.

DAY 4
SUGGESTED READING
MATTHEW 6:3 - 4

> **³ But when you give to the needy, do not let your left hand know what your right hand is doing,**
>
> **⁴ so that your giving may be in secret. Then your Father, who sees what is done in secret, will reward you. (NIV)**

There are those who make a big production of giving to the poor, those who want everyone to know that they are benevolent. This is prideful and a sin in God's eyes.

Giving is something that is personal and done from compassion. There is no need to showcase the poor that you are helping. They appreciate what you are doing.

God also knows of your duty and your work.

DAY 5
SUGGESTED READING
LUKE 3:11

**¹¹ John answered, "Anyone who has two shirts should share with the one who has none, and anyone who has food should do the same." (NIV)**

Be benevolent to the poor. If you have excess, be willing to give. This pertains to possessions, money or food.

Remember the commandant, "love thy neighbor". Giving when we can is an action that God enjoys.

*DAY 6*
*SUGGESTED READING*
*JAMES 2:15 – 16*

**¹⁵ Suppose a brother or a sister is without clothes and daily food.**

**¹⁶ If one of you says to them, "Go in peace; keep warm and well fed," but does nothing about their physical needs, what good is it? (NIV)**

Our brothers and sisters are fellow Christians. How could we ignore their need and think that we are faithful to the Lord? If we could treat a fellow Christian thus, how do we view the non-believer.

Consider how the Lord will view this action on judgement day.

DAY 7
SUGGESTED READING
ACTS 20:35

**³⁵ In everything I did, I showed you that by this kind of hard work we must help the weak, remembering the words the Lord Jesus himself said: 'It is more blessed to give than to receive.' (NIV)**

This is the character of Christ. He devoted his life to give to mankind. We to must try to do the same.

If we are truly affluent we should rejoice in the ability to give. We must give not only of our possessions but of our testimony to Christ. The poor need to know that the Lord loves them also, no matter their position in life.

# WEEK 18
# GOD'S CARE

DAY 1
SUGGESTED READING
PHILIPPIANS 4:19

**[19] But my God shall supply all your need according to his riches in glory by Christ Jesus. (KJV)**

God is infinite in his generosity to Christians. This is especially true when Christians are in need. God does not want us to suffer and is always there to help us.

Looking at the broader picture though, we need to understand that the principle is God's help when we help someone else.

So, be generous with others in need. Don't withhold surplus money thinking it will not be resupplied. God will reimburse your generosity.

*DAY 2*
*SUGGESTED READING*
*ISAIAH 46:4*

**⁴ Even to your old age and gray hairs
I am he, I am he who will sustain you.
I have made you and I will carry you;
I will sustain you and I will rescue you. (NIV)**

God will never forget his people. He has chosen us from the beginning and saw to it that we were saved by Christ. Unlike our earthly parents, he will be with us until we die. Age does not make us less dependent.

The Lord watches over our life and gives us guidance as Christians. He is there to listen to our problems and answer our prayers. He will not let us fail if we trust in Him.

The second message to this verse is analogous to the Jewish people. He declared them his chosen people and promised to be there for them, to take care of them and protect them from their enemies.

Though God promised to be there for the Jewish people, they turned their back on Jesus. Do not be like the Jewish people and cut Jesus out of your life. He will treat us in the same fashion.

*DAY 3*
*SUGGESTED READING*
*JOSHUA 1:8 – 9*

**⁸ Keep this Book of the Law always on your lips; meditate on it day and night, so that you may be careful to do everything written in it. Then you will be prosperous and successful.**

**⁹ Have I not commanded you? Be strong and courageous. Do not be afraid; do not be discouraged, for the LORD your God will be with you wherever you go." (NIV)**

In these verses, God tells Joshua what he needs to do to be successful. This also applies to all Christians today. Keeping God's word will reward you with success in all that you do. This is God's promise in this verse.

We must endeavor to read scripture daily. We must work diligently to memorize verses. This is not arduous work, but it does require diligence. Repetition is the key. Repeat verses throughout the day that you will be able to call upon them for yourself or proselytizing.

Studying the Bible will give you all the direction you need in life. The work put into this will provide you with greater insight to the will and mind of God. It is wise to study the Bible rather than seek the counsel of man, which we know can be flawed.

*DAY 4*
*SUGGESTED READING*
*LUKE 12:6 - 7*

**⁶ Are not five sparrows sold for two farthings, and not one of them is forgotten before God?**

**⁷ But even the very hairs of your head are all numbered. Fear not therefore: ye are of more value than many sparrows. (KJV)**

God is in constant awareness of every aspect of our life. In these verses, Jesus references sparrows, which are the least expensive and relatively worthless commodity in the markets. He makes the assertion that as insignificant as these birds are, God is sovereign over them.

If God cares about sparrows, he surely cares for us. Be strong in your faith to God. He will never leave us alone. He assures his disciples. He assures us.

DAY 5
SUGGESTED READING
1 PETER 5:7

**⁷ Casting all your care upon him; for he careth for you. (KJV)**

God wants us as Christians to turn to him when we have concerns in our life. Whether these concerns are spiritual or temporal, God is concerned.

The principle behind this verse is that we humble ourselves when we put our trust in God. We know that we should not trust in our own intelligences to solve our life's problems but to give our problem to God knowing that he will bear the majority of the burden.

Trust in the Lord and he will take care of you.

*DAY 6*
*SUGGESTED READING*
*MATTHEW 6:31 – 33*

**[31] Therefore do not be anxious, saying, 'What shall we eat?' or 'What shall we drink?' or 'What shall we wear?'**

**[32] For the Gentiles seek after all these things, and your heavenly Father knows that you need them all.**

**[33] But seek first the kingdom of God and his righteousness, and all these things will be added to you. (ESV)**

We must trust in the Lord above all else. This is difficult when we are concerned about not having the basic necessities for life. This is also a test of our faith. Our concerns arise when we see or hear of someone we know that has lost their job or for some other reason has happened upon financial rune.

Surely, we should pray for them but as Christians we should not worry for God has said he will take care of us. Jesus states, "do not be anxious" (Matthew 6:25 ESV). This is what we can base our trust. We are not being promised riches and should not expect as much. God knows exactly what we need.

Without these concerns, we must focus on what really is important, which is serving God and living for his glory. Be content for what is provided to us today. Worry about what you can control today and let the Lord take care of tomorrow. He will take care of us.

DAY 7
SUGGESTED READING
HEBREWS 13:5 - 6

**⁵ Keep your lives free from the love of money and be content with what you have, because God has said,**

**"Never will I leave you;
never will I forsake you."**

**⁶ So we say with confidence,**

**"The Lord is my helper; I will not be afraid. What can mere mortals do to me?" (NIV)**

Without doubt money is necessary for securing the needs to survive in todays world. Money is necessary to pay mortgage, bills, for food, for gas, for clothes, and cover any emergencies that may occur unexpectedly.

Christians, like anyone else struggle to keep money in perspective in daily life. With our society's value on money and the attainment of it, it is difficult not to be preoccupied by it. But keep in mind, Man cannot provide as the Lord can.

Paul tells us to be content with what we have. God knows what we need and will provide. He promised this to Christians back then and we can trust that it still applies. God will keep his promise to his people.

# WEEK 19
# GOD'S WILL

DAY 1
SUGGESTED READING
JEREMIAH 29:11

**¹¹ For I know the plans I have for you," declares the LORD, "plans to prosper you and not to harm you, plans to give you hope and a future. (NIV)**

One of the ideology's I live by is that, the past is the past, I can only control what I do today, the future is in God's hands. I believe that this is all any Christian can do. We surely can't change the past and we have no idea what tomorrow brings. Jesus tells us to do what we can today.

God tells us that he knows what is in store for our future. He tells us that we will have a bright future. It is comforting to know that the Lord is thinking about our future concerns. We can be relieved to know what to expect.

*DAY 2*
*SUGGESTED READING*
*1 THESSALONIANS 4:3*

**³ It is God's will that you should be sanctified: that you should avoid sexual immorality; (NIV)**

As a Christian, we are called to be holy. Separated from the non-believers to do the work of the Lord. This is what it means to be sanctified. This is the will of God.

As such, we are constrained for certain acts that are common among the non-believers. These acts are sins in the eyes of God. Sexual immorality is singled out as this is rampart in our society and is the ruin of many good people.

DAY 3
SUGGESTED READING
1 PETER 2:15

**¹⁵ For it is God's will that by doing good you should silence the ignorant talk of foolish people. (NIV)**

Christians must behave in a way that they cannot be spoken of in ill regard. Ignorant talk regarding them should be ignored because there is no basis for it if they are doing God's will.

God's will is to obey his laws. Let the non-believers observe this obedient behavior always that they cannot say bad things or spread lies about you.

Non-believers will always be critics of Christians. They criticize by knowing only half the story. Most of the time they do not want to hear the other half, God's half. Christians must maintain good behavior and a good testimony. This is the best defense against the intimidation of the non-believer.

DAY 4
SUGGESTED READING
JOHN 7:17

**¹⁷ If any man will do his will, he shall know of the doctrine, whether it be of God, or whether I speak of myself. (KJV)**

If a person wants to do the will of God, they will learn the lessons of the Bible. They will understand that they are of sinful nature and that they will need to be reborn through the grace of God and this requires an acceptance of Jesus as the savior.

Jesus tells us that we are to apply everything that we are told to what is required of us by God. If we hear anything that is contrary to the nature of God, we then know that it is from man. However, if what we hear is consistent with the nature of God we must take it to heart and apply it to our lives.

DAY 5
SUGGESTED READING
EPHESIANS 5:17 - 20

**[17] Therefore do not be foolish, but understand what the Lord's will is.**

**[18] Do not get drunk on wine, which leads to debauchery. Instead, be filled with the Spirit,**

**[19] speaking to one another with psalms, hymns, and songs from the Spirit. Sing and make music from your heart to the Lord,**

**[20] always giving thanks to God the Father for everything, in the name of our Lord Jesus Christ. (NIV)**

Christians should always be aware of how they are perceived in the eyes of the non-believers. The non-believer is constantly looking for ways to criticize Christians and call them hypocrites.

Therefore, it is important to thoroughly understand the will of God. Know that God wants that we remain sober, chaste, holy and pure. Exhibiting these qualities at all times makes it hard for anyone to speak ill of you.

*DAY 6*
*SUGGESTED READING*
*JOHN 6:38 – 40*

**[38] For I have come down from heaven not to do my will but to do the will of him who sent me.**

**[39] And this is the will of him who sent me, that I shall lose none of all those he has given me but raise them up at the last day.**

**[40] For my Father's will is that everyone who looks to the Son and believes in him shall have eternal life, and I will raise them up at the last day."**
**(NIV)**

This verse explains the will of God and the purpose of Jesus coming to man.

Jesus explains that he is sent from heaven to do the will of God, which is to claim all he had been given.

It is also stated that the will of God is to grant the gift of eternal life to all that believes in Jesus.

DAY 7
SUGGESTED READING
JOHN 9:31

**³¹ We know that God does not listen to sinners, but if anyone is a worshiper of God and does his will, God listens to him. (ESV)**

This verse implies that God will not listen to bad people. However, what it is really is saying is that God will not listen to anyone who is a non-believer.

This is important to those who believe their good works will get them into heaven. They couldn't be farther from the truth. God does not listen to their prayers

To the followers of his Law, God listens. He encourages us to bring our prayers to him and trust him to answer them.

# WEEK 20
# GRACE

DAY 1
SUGGESTED READING
HEBREWS 4:16

**¹⁶ Let us have confidence, then, and approach God's throne, where there is grace. There we will receive mercy and find grace to help us just when we need it. (GNT)**

The throne of grace is that special place where it is recognized as a place of reverence. To come to the throne of grace is to seek the mercy of God and find grace to help in the time of need.

Approach the throne of grace with humility and be prepared to ask for help in faith, not doubting but trusting in the promises of God to his servant. You should approach with confidence as you have Jesus as your mediator.

*DAY 2*
*SUGGESTED READING*
*ACTS 6:8 - 10*

> **⁸ Now Stephen, a man full of God's grace and power, performed great wonders and signs among the people.**
>
> **⁹ Opposition arose, however, from members of the Synagogue of the Freedmen (as it was called)— Jews of Cyrene and Alexandria as well as the provinces of Cilicia and Asia—who began to argue with Stephen.**
>
> **¹⁰ But they could not stand up against the wisdom the Spirit gave him as he spoke. (NIV)**

Stephen was a highly educated man who was selected by the disciples to spread the gospel of Jesus. Because of his faith and belief, he was graced by God with great understanding and ability. As a result, he was able to perform "great wonders and signs".

We to as Christians are graced with ability. As we learn and grow in our faith, our abilities will increase. There is no limit to what we can attain through faith. We are given everything we need in the Bible to face any challenges.

DAY 3
SUGGESTED READING
ROMANS 3:20 – 24

**²⁰ Therefore no one will be declared righteous in God's sight by the works of the law; rather, through the law we become conscious of our sin.**

**²¹ But now apart from the law the righteousness of God has been made known, to which the Law and the Prophets testify.**

**²² This righteousness is given through faith in[a] Jesus Christ to all who believe. There is no difference between Jew and Gentile,**

**²³ for all have sinned and fall short of the glory of God,**

**²⁴ and all are justified freely by his grace through the redemption that came by Christ Jesus. (NIV)**

All have sinned in the eyes of God. This is from the original sin of Adam. The Law cannot protect us from this sin because it has no power to justify. The Law only exposes the nature of the sin.

There is nothing that we can do to work off the sin. We are all guilty before God.

It is only by the grace of God through Jesus that we can be cleansed of our sins.

DAY 4
SUGGESTED READING
EPHESIANS 2:4 - 9

> **⁴ But because of his great love for us, God, who is rich in mercy,**
>
> **⁵ made us alive with Christ even when we were dead in transgressions—it is by grace you have been saved.**
>
> **⁶ And God raised us up with Christ and seated us with him in the heavenly realms in Christ Jesus,**
>
> **⁷ in order that in the coming ages he might show the incomparable riches of his grace, expressed in his kindness to us in Christ Jesus.**
>
> **⁸ For it is by grace you have been saved, through faith—and this is not from yourselves, it is the gift of God—**
>
> **⁹ not by works, so that no one can boast. (NIV)**

Those who work hard at being good people or giving donations but have not accepted Christ will not be saved. Even the sinful can do this. Still most people believe that salvation is conditional.

Salvation starts with faith. Without faith there is no salvation. If one believes, they become saved by the grace of God. This is a free gift spawned from love.

God offers salvation to everyone. Don't let anyone believe that just because they are good they are justified. This would give an unfair advantage to the wealthy and influential. It would also give them a means to boast of their salvation.

*DAY 5*
*SUGGESTED READING*
*EPHESIANS 4:7*

**⁷ But unto every one of us is given grace according to the measure of the gift of Christ. (KJV)**

Christ is given the authority to allocate special abilities to those who believe in him. This is not given as a reward for works but as a gift of grace from God.

Grace is a blessing that is given by God and is bestowed upon Christians. But since all Christians are different, the gifts given are at the discretion of Christ to be used to fulfill one's function for the Lord.

Every Christian is given enough grace to live a life of holiness.

DAY 6
SUGGESTED READING
HEBREWS 13:9

> **⁹ Do not be carried away by all kinds of strange teachings. It is good for our hearts to be strengthened by grace, not by eating ceremonial foods, which is of no benefit to those who do so. (NIV)**

Paul tells believers not to be influenced by other beliefs and opinions. They may be older beliefs or even similar to the truth. He cautions us that the bringer of these messages may be from respected leaders that may have been led astray.

Strengthen your foundation in the grace of the Lord. Understand that this grace teaches us the truth of Gods pure religion. Be confident in your faith. Do not be easily swayed or tempted to listen to new or alternate positions.

*DAY 7*
*SUGGESTED READING*
*1 PETER 4:10*

**¹⁰ Each of you should use whatever gift you have received to serve others, as faithful stewards of God's grace in its various forms. (NIV)**

Every Christian has been given a spiritual gift by God. These gifts are free by the grace of God. As such, we exercise our gift in grace because it was given to us in grace. Spiritual gifts enable the Holy Spirit to work within and through us. These gifts are unique to each of us as Christians.

Understand that "Gift" is given to us by the grace of God. It is a free gift. We did not earn it. We did not pay for it. There is nothing we need to do but accept it. God gives it to us freely because he loves us.

God wants us to use the gifts we are given. Every Christian is instructed to do use their gifts without exception. To not use the gift is an insult to God and he warns us not to neglect the gifts.

# WEEK 21
# HEAVEN

DAY 1
SUGGESTED READING
MATTHEW 7:13 – 14

**¹³ "Enter through the narrow gate. For wide is the gate and broad is the road that leads to destruction, and many enter through it.**

**¹⁴ But small is the gate and narrow the road that leads to life, and only a few find it. (NIV)**

It is easy to get distracted from the right way to live our lives. This could be intentional with willingness to sin or through commitments to work or others that take away our focus from Christ.

Yes, the road is narrow, and the gate is small that leads to heaven. Without Christ in our life it is impossible to find.

*DAY 2*
*SUGGESTED READING*
*JOHN 14.2*

**² In my Father's house are many mansions: if it were not so, I would have told you. I go to prepare a place for you. (KJV)**

Jesus reassures his disciples that their efforts in faith are not in vain. He tells them to rest assure that they will have a place in heaven.

All Christians have this to look forward too. This verse is a promise from Christ. How wonderful is that? When we are feeling gloomy in this earthly life or are approaching the end of our life, we too can rest assure that there is a place in heaven for us after death.

DAY 3
SUGGESTED READING
REVELATION 22:1 - 5

**¹ Then the angel showed me the river of the water of life, as clear as crystal, flowing from the throne of God and of the Lamb**

**² down the middle of the great street of the city. On each side of the river stood the tree of life, bearing twelve crops of fruit, yielding its fruit every month. And the leaves of the tree are for the healing of the nations.**

**³ No longer will there be any curse. The throne of God and of the Lamb will be in the city, and his servants will serve him.**

**⁴ They will see his face, and his name will be on their foreheads.**

**⁵ There will be no more night. They will not need the light of a lamp or the light of the sun, for the Lord God will give them light. And they will reign for ever and ever. (NIV)**

Here we are given a glimpse of heaven. Imagine a place of extreme purity where there are no blemishes or imperfections.

Here is the throne of God and Jesus. Here we can serve him in all his glory.

This is the City of God. It is Eden restored. The river of life flows through it. The tree of life resides beside it.

*DAY 4*
*SUGGESTED READING*
*1 CORINTHIANS 2:7 – 9*

**⁷ No, we declare God's wisdom, a mystery that has been hidden and that God destined for our glory before time began.**

**⁸ None of the rulers of this age understood it, for if they had, they would not have crucified the Lord of glory.**

**⁹ However, as it is written:**

**"What no eye has seen,
what no ear has heard,
and what no human mind has conceived"—
the things God has prepared for those who love him— (NIV)**

God had a plan for believers then as he does for believers today. And like the rulers of that time, God's plan is not plain to the rulers of today. Certain events will not be revealed before it's right time.

Christians have knowledge of God's plan because of the gospel of Christ but cannot imagine what God truly has in mind. What we as Christians can hold onto is the fact that whatever the mystery of God is, it is for the betterment of our earthly life and how glorious our eternal life will be.

DAY 5
SUGGESTED READING
RELELATION 21:21 - 25

**²¹ The twelve gates were twelve pearls, each gate made of a single pearl. The great street of the city was of gold, as pure as transparent glass.**

**²² I did not see a temple in the city, because the Lord God Almighty and the Lamb are its temple.**

**²³ The city does not need the sun or the moon to shine on it, for the glory of God gives it light, and the Lamb is its lamp.**

**²⁴ The nations will walk by its light, and the kings of the earth will bring their splendor into it.**

**²⁵ On no day will its gates ever be shut, for there will be no night there. (NIV)**

These verses give us another glimpse of heaven. The description is a fantastic vision which most likely is not accurate but is the best that John could give given his experience and vocabulary.

Regardless, the description obviously portrays a heaven of great beauty and majesty. There is no other place ever conceived nor shall be. All the materials described are those that do not tarnish or fade.

DAY 6
SUGGESTED READING
REVELATION 21:1 - 5

¹ Then I saw "a new heaven and a new earth," for the first heaven and the first earth had passed away, and there was no longer any sea.

² I saw the Holy City, the new Jerusalem, coming down out of heaven from God, prepared as a bride beautifully dressed for her husband.

³ And I heard a loud voice from the throne saying, "Look! God's dwelling place is now among the people, and he will dwell with them. They will be his people, and God himself will be with them and be their God.

⁴ 'He will wipe every tear from their eyes. There will be no more death' or mourning or crying or pain, for the old order of things has passed away."

⁵ He who was seated on the throne said, "I am making everything new!" Then he said, "Write this down, for these words are trustworthy and true." (NIV)

The current heaven and earth will pass away. This paves the way to a new heaven and earth. We cannot conceive of how things are created by God. All we can know is that God tells us what he will do, and we have faith that his promises are incontestable.

He also tells us that those who are believers will be comforted. That everything will be new and good. Prepare ourselves. Keep focused on the Law and on Christ.

DAY 7
SUGGESTED READING
RELEVALTIONS 21:27

**$^{27}$ Nothing impure will ever enter it, nor will anyone who does what is shameful or deceitful, but only those whose names are written in the Lamb's book of life. (NIV)**

Heaven is a place for only it's exclusive members. We, Christians, are obviously the members. We have accepted Christ as our personal savior. We have studied hard his Word to understand the grace given to us. We have followed the Law of the Lord to be righteous in his eyes. We struggled through our Earthly lives waiting for God's time.

How horrible it is to be excluded though? Those who chose not to believe will now witness the folly of their ways. For those unsaved by the blood of Christ will forever be denied access to Heaven. Their names shall not be in the Book of Life.

Not only will unforgiven Sin keep you out of Heaven but even the tendency for Sin prevent admission. This is not for debate. This is a declaration from God as he cannot tolerate anything that is of sinful nature.

# WEEK 22
# HOLY SPIRIT

DAY 1
SUGGESTED READING
ACTS 2:38

**³⁸ Then Peter said unto them, Repent, and be baptized every one of you in the name of Jesus Christ for the remission of sins, and ye shall receive the gift of the Holy Ghost. (KJV)**

Peter explains what happens after one repents and is baptized. Once Christ cleanses us of sin our bodies are fit to receive the Holy Spirit.

This Holy Spirit is from God and until one repents he cannot receive it. The Holy Spirit sustains our soul and allows us the gifts that have been allotted by God.

*DAY 2*
*SUGGESTED READING*
*JOHN 14:26*

**²⁶ The Helper, the Holy Spirit, whom the Father will send in my name, will teach you everything and make you remember all that I have told you. (GNT)**

We are reminded that Jesus will not be with us forever. In his stead God will grant us a spirit to sustain us. This is important for the remembrance of the teachings we have acquired.

The Bible is a comprehensive manuscript that is difficult to memorize. The Holy Spirit will help us to remember important topics that can be used in our proselytizing and spiritual growth. The stronger our faith, the more enabled the Holy Spirit will be. Keeping in touch with the Holy Spirit during the day, through prayer, will allow the Spirit to guide us.

DAY 3
SUGGESTED READING
ISAIAH 11:2

> **² And the spirit of the Lord shall rest upon him,**
> **the spirit of wisdom and understanding,**
> **the spirit of counsel and might,**
> **the spirit of knowledge and of the fear of the Lord; (KJV)**

John describes the gifts of the Holy Spirit in Jesus. These gifts are given by God and are the endowments that he lived his life by and that we, as his disciples, are to live by also.

The Holy Spirit is given to each of us who have accepted Jesus as our savior. God equips us with the Holy Spirit to go out and minister to the masses.

It is hard to fathom that something that applies to Jesus could possibly apply to us but think of this. The Holy Spirit was given to Jesus upon his baptism. This is the same baptism by the Holy Spirit that Christians receive. The Holy Spirit, initially given to Jesus's disciples, is given to all who believe in Jesus and is the spiritual mark that is characteristic of God's people.

*DAY 4*
*SUGGESTED READING*
*2 CORINTHIANS 3:17*

## ¹⁷ Now the Lord is that Spirit: and where the Spirit of the Lord is, there is liberty. (KJV)

In the Old Testament, the Lord is considered to be God. In the New Testament, the Lord is considered to be Jesus. The Holy Spirit is part of the Trinity which is the essence of God and Jesus in spirit form. The Holy Spirit is real as God and Jesus and plays a vital role in our development as Christians and communication with God.

It has been said that Jesus is the Spirit of Christianity. Through Jesus we are saved. Through Jesus we can ask help from God. We are given the Holy Spirit when we receive Jesus as Lord and savior.

This verse reminds us that if we are filled with the Holy Spirit, we are freed from ignorance of the gospel, freed from the bondage of Satan, freed from eternal damnation and Hell, freed to have access to God

DAY 5
SUGGESTED READING
EZEKIEL 36:26 - 27

**[26] A new heart also will I give you, and a new spirit will I put within you: and I will take away the stony heart out of your flesh, and I will give you a heart of flesh.**

**[27] And I will put my spirit within you, and cause you to walk in my statutes, and ye shall keep my judgments, and do them. (KJV)**

The unsaved heart is hardened to the ways of righteousness. It belongs to Satan and is prone to sin. It lacks a moral barometer and will have great difficulty in living the righteous life.

Christians are given a new heart and a new spirit. The new spirit is the Holy Spirit which gives God access to our soul. This access allows us to receive the Law of the Lord and changes our heart to act in a moral and righteous manner.

*DAY 6*
*SUGGESTED READING*
*JOHN 14:16 -17*

**¹⁶ And I will ask the Father, and he will give you another advocate to help you and be with you forever—**

**¹⁷ the Spirit of truth. The world cannot accept him, because it neither sees him nor knows him. But you know him, for he lives with you and will be in you. (NIV)**

The Holy Spirit is the power of God. Jesus ask God to send the Holy Spirit to abide in us as Christians because he is not here in physical form.

The Holy Spirit allows Christians to be in direct contact with God and Jesus. Through the Holy Spirit we are able to use the gifts that were given to Jesus in our ministering. The world of the unbelievers has no access to God's blessings and therefore cannot appreciate the Holy Spirit.

DAY 7
SUGGESTED READING
JOHN 20:21 - 23

> **²¹ Again Jesus said, "Peace be with you! As the Father has sent me, I am sending you."**
>
> **²² And with that he breathed on them and said, "Receive the Holy Spirit.**
>
> **²³ If you forgive anyone's sins, their sins are forgiven; if you do not forgive them, they are not forgiven." (NIV)**

Jesus is telling his disciples that they are to go out and save peoples souls. To be clear, they are not given the power to forgive, for this is only for God or Jesus to do, but to preach the means by which one can be saved.

Like the disciples of old, we too are admonished to go out and preach the gospel of Christ. This was his last command to his disciples and is our mission also. We are crucified in Christ and live with the Holy Spirit within us. We are not to assume the power of forgiveness for ourselves but must tell people that if they believe in Christ message their sins will be forgiven and the Holy Spirit will enter into them.

If they do not receive the truth they are being told, their sins will not be forgiven. This non-acceptance comes with consequences. "Whoever believes in the Son has eternal life, but whoever rejects the Son will not see life, for God's wrath remains on him" (John 3:36 NIV).

# WEEK 23
# HUMILITY

DAY 1
SUGGESTED READING
PHILIPPIANS 2:7

## ⁷ But made himself of no reputation, and took upon him the form of a servant, and was made in the likeness of men: (KIV)

"For you know the grace of our Lord Jesus Christ that though He was rich, yet for your sakes He became poor, that you through His poverty might become rich." (2 Cor. 8:9 NIV) Jesus did not have to give up his deity but how he preach humility if he didn't.

Jesus showed what it is to be humble by taking on the form of man and becoming mortal. He was born poor with no title or position in the eyes of man. He lived his whole life in poverty and suffering. He never tried to be something greater than that of a servant. He died being hated by the people for no reason but for teaching the truth of God.

We spend our whole life trying to build a reputation. We pride ourselves in the honor we have amongst our peers. This sin of pride can cause us to stray from righteousness. When we start feeling that we need recognition and praise for our accomplishments, we need to remember how Jesus presented himself. Humility makes us equal with our fellow man.

*DAY 2*
*SUGGESTED READING*
*PROVERBS 16:19*

**¹⁹ Better it is to be of an humble spirit with the lowly, than to divide the spoil with the proud. (KJV)**

The Beatitudes tells us, "Blessed are the meek for they will inherit the Earth" (Matthew 5:5 NIV). As Jesus was meek and lowly, we to as Christians should follow his example. Being of humble spirit will keep us from the sin of Pride.

The followers of Jesus who humble themselves before God will receive the gifts of God. It is difficult to be humble and not complain in a world where the proud are always looking for ways to suppress others to gain more power. They do this to have others look to them as great leaders among man.

Those who fake humility to elevate their status are condemning themselves to Hell. When I watch the many religious channels available, I see the proud talk about how great their ministries are. I listen for content to their message and all I hear is a plea for money. Some will disguise this plea by asking one to but their books and tapes. It angers me that these "proud" religious leaders aren't even ashamed of their hypocrisy. La Rochefoucald wrote in 1665; "Humility is often only feigned submission which people use to render others submissive. It is a subterfuge of pride which lowers itself in order to rise."

It is better to follow Jesus in his humility than it is to risk one's eternal soul to the sin of Pride.

DAY 3
SUGGESTED READING
COLOSSIANS 3:12

**¹² Therefore, as God's chosen people, holy and dearly loved, clothe yourselves with compassion, kindness, humility, gentleness and patience. (NIV)**

Christians are the chosen of God. As such we learn from the Bible our responsibilities in this corrupt world. Reading this verse tells us the way we should conduct our lives. It is a growing process that requires work daily.

Keep in mind that these attributes are the same found in the behaviour of Jesus. He has set the standard that we must try and achieve. Pray for wisdom and perseverance and keep focusing on doing good. God will hear you and strengthen the spirit within you.

DAY 4
SUGGESTED READING
1 PETER 5:5

**⁵ In the same way, you who are younger, submit yourselves to your elders. All of you, clothe yourselves with humility toward one another, because,**

**"God opposes the proud but shows favor to the humble." (NIV)**

It is natural when we are young to be proud of what we are accomplishing. The young have always felt that they are in control of every situation. We know this because we have been through the same process as they.

We must remind them how Christ was humble in his life and how he respected his elders. Respect towards elders will earn their respect in return. Always remind the young it is better to be humble and serve for pride is a subtle sin that will grow and destroy one's soul.

DAY 5
SUGGESTED READING
PSALM 23:9

**⁹ He guides the humble in what is right
and teaches them his way. (NIV)**

It is impossible for the proud person to be taught because he already feels that he knows it all. The proud have no respect for the knowledge of others. The proud will not get into heaven.

To learn the righteous way of the Lord requires one to humble themselves and give up their pride. Being humble will allow the Holy Spirit to enter one's body and accept the teachings of Jesus.

The humble want to learn. They no longer trust their prideful selves. If one's mind has turned to the Lord for guidance their souls will be at peace

*DAY 6*
*SUGGESTED READING*
*JAMES 4:6*

**⁶ But he gives us more grace. That is why Scripture says:**

**"God opposes the proud
but shows favor to the humble." (NIV)**

God does for us Christians what the world cannot. He gives us more grace. What form of grace is determined by what He feels we need. It may be more happiness. It may be more money. It may be better health. Regardless, because of the presence of the Holy Spirit that resides within us we are granted more grace.

Guard yourself against pride though. Pride will make one admire himself more than the creator who gave them their gifts. Pride makes a person believe in themselves and causes them to think they don't need anyone else to help them.

Be humble before God. Confess your sins and ask for forgiveness. Do not be proud. Pray to be a servant to your fellow man and the Lord will bestow his favors upon you.

DAY 7
SUGGESTED READING
PROVERBS 22:4

**⁴ Humility is the fear of the Lord;
its wages are riches and honor and life. (NIV)**

To be reverent of the Lord we must be humble. This is the righteous way. Not only must we be humble to the Lord, we must be humble to our fellow man. Honor God in all you do. Be willing to serve whomever needs help or support. Sacrifice of yourself without expectations of reward.

There are rewards though and they are promised by God. We will be compensated with spiritual riches that cannot be given to us by any in this world.

# WEEK 24
# JUSTICE

*DAY 1*
*SUGGESTED READING*
*ECLESIASTES 3:17*

**¹⁷ I said to myself,**

**"God will bring into judgment
both the righteous and the wicked,
for there will be a time for every activity,
a time to judge every deed." (NIV)**

Justice is given only by God. God will meter judgement based on the way we conducted our life. On Judgement Day, all will come before the throne of God and be judged.

There will be no doubt about the judgement given. God is just and cannot judge falsely or wrongly. The righteous will have no fear of the time of judgement.

*DAY 2*
*SUGGESTED READING*
*ISAIAH 56:1 - 2*

**¹This is what the L<small>ORD</small> says:**

**"Maintain justice
and do what is right,
for my salvation is close at hand
and my righteousness will soon be revealed.
² Blessed is the one who does this—
the person who holds it fast,
who keeps the Sabbath without desecrating it,
and keeps their hands from doing any evil." (NIV)**

God gives us his expectations in these verses. It pertains to what we owe to one another and to God.

God tells us that Judgement Day is coming soon, so resist sin and keep holy.

DAY 3
SUGGESTED READING
JEREMIAH 22:3

> **³ This is what the LORD says: Do what is just and right. Rescue from the hand of the oppressor the one who has been robbed. Do no wrong or violence to the foreigner, the fatherless or the widow, and do not shed innocent blood in this place. (NIV)**

The Lord want us to be righteous in all that we do. Always think in terms of what is just. If we use this as a barometer then our actions will be right.

Endeavor to do no wrong. We cannot always be good, but we should always work hard to develop a pattern of goodness. Understand that others are subject to sinful behavior and be patient with them. Try and lead them to right thinking and repentance. Then they may start to lead a just life.

*DAY 4*
*SUGGESTED READING*
*PSALM 140:12*

## **¹² I know that the LORD will maintain the cause of the afflicted, and the right of the poor. (KJV)**

Throughout the Bible there is mention of how God will take care of the poor. The poor then, as now, are subject to less privilege and less justice. The Lord is the only real refuge for the poor.

But not only the poor, but for all those who are persecuted in the name of the Lord. The evil will try to do bad things to those who follow the Law of the Lord. They will say dreadful things about them. This is spoken of by Jesus in the Sermon of the Mount where he states that, "the prophets were persecuted before you".

The Lord will always take up the cause of the poor. More important though, is that the Lord will not change his justice. If the cause warrants justice, God will always take the side of right.

DAY 5
SUGGESTED READING
DEUTERONOMY 32:4

**⁴ He is the Rock, his works are perfect,
and all his ways are just.
A faithful God who does no wrong,
upright and just is he. (NIV)**

This is the first time in the Bible that God is referred to as The Rock. This reference represents the foundation of Gods philosophy which cannot be changed or moved. Metaphorically, The Rock denotes divine power, faithfulness and love. These are the same attributes that Jesus portrayed in his life and gospel.

Because God is perfect, his words and actions are true and just. This cannot waver or change ever, or he would not be perfect. His justice comes from flawless wisdom. The Bible gives us his word. We just need to trust him.

DAY 6
SUGGESTED READING
PROVERBS 21:15

**¹⁵ When justice is done, it brings joy to the righteous
but terror to evildoers. (NIV)**

The righteous person enjoys seeing justice done. They also derive pleasure in practicing it in their lives. The righteous know they are doing the will of God and that pleases both God and themselves.

The person who practices sin is in fear of justice. They know that they have done wrong and are always trying to avoid judgement.

DAY 7
SUGGESTED READING
MICAH 6:8

> **⁸ He has shown you, O mortal, what is good.**
> **And what does the L**ORD **require of you?**
> **To act justly and to love mercy**
> **and to walk humbly with your God. (NIV)**

God has given us his Law. He has told us to follow them faithfully. We must study every aspect of the Law and keep them in our hearts that we do not break them.

He wants us to recognize what is just and apply it to our life with love and mercy. We must realize that everything that we accomplish is through the grace of God and that by being humble towards God and to our fellow man will see all as equal. We will be impartial when we deal with both the rich and the poor.

As stated, we must be humble to walk with God. We must keep God on our mind constantly during the day and let him guide us. Trust in the Lord and not our own devices. Our wisdom is flawed and the more we try to direct our life, the more difficulties we will encounter.

# WEEK 25
# LOVE

## DAY 1
## SUGGESTED READING
## 1 CORINTHIANS 13:4 - 5

**[4] Love is patient, love is kind. It does not envy, it does not boast, it is not proud.**

**[5] It does not dishonor others, it is not self-seeking, it is not easily angered, it keeps no record of wrongs. (NIV)**

Paul tells the Corinthians that the use of their spiritual gifts is ineffective if not done in love. They were using their gifts apart from love. This love should be selfless and should be a priority for every Christian.

It is difficult to love everyone when so many are not feeling the same for you. People get emotional and impatient with others and don't feel like loving. But Paul tells us that Love should not be an emotion. He tells us that Love is an action to be experienced and demonstrated.

*DAY 2*
*SUGGESTED READING*
*PROVERBS 3:3 - 4*

**³ Let love and faithfulness never leave you;
bind them around your neck,
write them on the tablet of your heart.**

**⁴ Then you will win favor and a good name
in the sight of God and man. (NIV)**

The righteous is always seeking the favor of God. They are inclined to study the Bible to learn its truths. Love and Faithfulness (Mercy and Truth) is what God requires of Christians. These are commanding principles that are to be committed to our heart.

There is a hidden warning here though. We should always seek favor from God. But be wary of seeking favor from man. Examine your motives and be sure that you are not putting man before God. Trust in God to guide you in your decisions.

DAY 3
SUGGESTED READING
1 JOHN 4:16

**¹⁶ We have come to know and believe the love God has for us. God is love. If you live in love, you live by the help of God and God lives in you. (NIV)**

In this verse John is making a declaration of truth. He states the relationship between God's love and that of us Believers. If we live in love for God, his love will be in us.

No matter what trials we encounter in this earthly life, God's love is there to be our refuge. We know this because when we accept God into our heart, his love is also accepted.

With love, show the unbeliever that they cannot experience the love of God without first knowing the love of God and then believing the love of God. A love that is unconditional and incomparable in that he sacrificed his son, Jesus, for our sins.

*DAY 4*
*SUGGESTED READING*
*1 CORINTHIANS 13:13*

**¹³ And now these three remain: faith, hope and love. But the greatest of these is love. (NIV)**

Paul tells us about the 3 gifts that God gives us as Christians. These gifts are spiritual and are given by the grace of God. Once given, these gifts are ours for this life and the next.

Faith is an active belief and trust in God.

Hope is the knowledge that God will do good things for us.

Love is a feeling from God which is profoundly tender and passionate. This love changes us as Christians as we give up selfish desires and endeavor to help others. This is the love God gives and is the greatest of God's gifts.

DAY 5
SUGGESTED READING
JOHN 15:12

> **¹² This is my commandment, That ye love one another, as I have loved you. (KJV)**

The Old Testament gives us the 10 Commandments. These were the Laws of the Lord that we were admonished to live our lives by.

1. You shall have no other gods before Me
2. "You shall not make for yourself a carved image, or any likeness of anything that is in heaven above, or that is in the earth beneath, or that is in the water under the earth; you shall not bow down to them nor serve them
3. "You shall not take the name of the Lord your God in vain, for the Lord will not hold him guiltless who takes His name in vain.
4. "Remember the Sabbath day, to keep it holy.
5. "Honor your father and your mother, that your days may be long upon the land which the Lord your God is giving you.
6. "You shall not murder.
7. "You shall not commit adultery.
8. "You shall not steal.
9. "You shall not bear false witness against your neighbor.
10. "You shall not covet your neighbor's house; you shall not covet your neighbor's wife, nor his male servant, nor his female servant, nor his ox, nor his donkey, nor anything that is your neighbor's."

*In the New Testament, Jesus gives us new commandments. The first and greatest commandment is:*

- "Love the Lord your God with all your heart and with all your soul and with all your mind" (Matthew 22:37 NIV)

The second is similar and all the commandants fall under it.

- "Love your neighbor as yourself." (Matthew 22:39 NIV)

Jesus commands us to love one another which is the paramount duty of Christians. It leads to servitude. This is how God loves us.

DAY 6
SUGGESTED READING
1 JOHN 4:8

## **⁸ Whoever does not love does not know God, because God is love. (NIV)**

How sad is it not to know true love? One who doesn't love God does not know him. This is a dangerous position to be in. They do not benefit from the graces that God bestows on us who do love him. Most importantly they have no chance to get into heaven.

God's love is just without hate. If hate was involved, then it would not be love. It is available for the believer or the unbeliever. God's love is proven in the fact that he sacrificed his son so that all could be saved.

The choice is there to know God and know his love.

*DAY 7*
*SUGGESTED READING*
*PSALM 116:1 - 2*

> **¹ I love the Lord, for he heard my voice;**
> **he heard my cry for mercy.**
> **² Because he turned his ear to me,**
> **I will call on him as long as I live. (NIV)**

There are times when our troubles are overwhelming. Times when we may be in a situation that we have no control. It is times like this God tells us to bring our problems to him in prayer.

God is listening when we pray. He knows our thoughts and hears our words. He knows what is best for us and wants good for us.

> ⁵ Trust in the Lord with all your heart
> and lean not on your own understanding;
> ⁶ in all your ways submit to him,
> and he will make your paths straight. (Proverbs 3:5-6 NIV)

God will answer our prayers. This is a promise he made to us. It may not be the exact answer that we want but you can trust that it is what God feels is best for us. He does this out of love.

# WEEK 26
# PRAISE

DAY 1
SUGGESTED READING
PSALM 150:1 – 6

> ¹ **Praise the LORD.**
> **Praise God in his sanctuary;**
> **praise him in his mighty heavens.**
>
> ² **Praise him for his acts of power;**
> **praise him for his surpassing greatness.**
>
> ³ **Praise him with the sounding of the trumpet,**
> **praise him with the harp and lyre,**
>
> ⁴ **praise him with timbrel and dancing,**
> **praise him with the strings and pipe,**
>
> ⁵ **praise him with the clash of cymbals,**
> **praise him with resounding cymbals.**
>
> ⁶ **Let everything that has breath praise the LORD.**
>
> **Praise the LORD. (NIV)**

The message here is simple. Every person alive should praise God. I don't think that "everything" in verse 6 pertains to animals, but surely, to all people. He is to be praised in Heaven and Earth. He should be praised for his power and greatness.

These verses praise him 13 times for what is to be believed by the Jewish scholars for his 13 attributes. These attributes were described by Torah (verses), according to the Talmud, were given to Moses by God after the people chose to worship a Golden Calf they made. Moses felt that this sin was beyond redemption. It is here the God spoke to Moses saying, "Whenever Israel sins, let them recite this [the Thirteen Attributes] in its proper order and I will forgive them."

DAY 2
SUGGESTED READING
HEBREW 13:15

> **¹⁵ Through Jesus, therefore, let us continually offer to God a sacrifice of praise—the fruit of lips that openly profess his name. (NIV)**

Everything we do as Christians is "through Christ". It follows that we should praise God through Christ. Not only should we praise him, but we should praise Him continuously. We should tell everyone of our praise without regret.

But why is this a sacrifice? Before Christ there was animal and harvest sacrifice. This was for atonement from God. Once Christ arrived there was no longer a need for the Jewish sacrificial forms. God wants us to sacrifice of self and he tells us that it is in the form of praise for the gift of Christ.

*DAY 3*
*SUGGESTED READING*
*ISAIAH 25:1*

> **¹ Lord, you are my God;**
> **I will exalt you and praise your name,**
> **for in perfect faithfulness**
> **you have done wonderful things,**
> **things planned long ago. (NIV)**

Always acknowledge that God is your personal Lord. For this praise him above all else. Be thankful that among all the things that God planned before the world came into existence, that you were chosen to be one of his children.

Give praise to God for being faithful to us. This includes his dependability, reliability and truthfulness. And most importantly, he sacrificed his son that we should be saved from our sins.

DAY 4
SUGGESTED READING
2 CORINTHIANS 1:3 - 4

**³ Praise be to the God and Father of our Lord Jesus Christ, the Father of compassion and the God of all comfort,**

**⁴ who comforts us in all our troubles, so that we can comfort those in any trouble with the comfort we ourselves receive from God. (NIV)**

All comfort comes from God. This is not an earthly comfort that is temporary but a satisfying comfort that is deep within the soul. This comfort gives peace to a troubled conscious or a broken spirit. It can ease anger and prevent hate. We can trust in this comfort as God is compassion.

The comfort that God provides is one that can be shared. When we see others that are troubled, we can share the message of God that will bring comfort if accepted.

Gods comfort creates a personal bond between one and God. It can be relied upon at any time. It is felt deep within the heart and soul. It is worthy of daily praise.

*DAY 5*
*SUGGESTED READING*
*1 CHRONICLES 29:11*

**¹¹ Yours, Lord, is the greatness and the power
and the glory and the majesty and the splendor,
for everything in heaven and earth is yours.
Yours, Lord, is the kingdom;
you are exalted as head over all. (NIV)**

This verse explains the sovereignty of God. He is the ruler of all things in Heaven and on Earth.

It may seem that Satan has substantial power over man and thing earthly, but his power is only allowed through the acquiescence of God. It is God who is the Almighty and has the plan for the universe.

God is to be praised for everything that he has created. To look upon his work is beyond comprehension in its grandeur.

DAY 6
SUGGESTED READING
PSALM 105:1

**¹ Give praise to the Lord, proclaim his name;
make known among the nations what he has done.
(NIV)**

The Lord has done many things for us as Christians. He has delivered us from evil and sin and gave us salvation. The Lord gives us gifts that enhance our spirit. Gifts that improve our knowledge of His love.

The Lord deserves our praise. We should tell everyone that we know and encounter about how He has changed our lives. We must tell everyone what his plan is for the world and those who believe in him.

*DAY 7*
*SUGGESTED READING*
*DANIEL 4:37*

**³⁷ Now I, Nebuchadnezzar, praise and exalt and glorify the King of heaven, because everything he does is right and all his ways are just. And those who walk in pride he is able to humble. (NIV)**

This is an interesting verse. Even though Nebuchadnezzar acknowledges the righteousness and justice of God he chooses to believe that his accomplishments are of his own doing. He does not believe that God played any part in his success.

Because of his pride, God caused an insanity in him for 7 years. In the end his mind restored, he finally acknowledged God's sovereignty and was restored to his throne.

God is righteous and just. He wants us to accept his grace. In order for this to occur, we must be humble. Pride is a sin that God will not tolerate. Pray that pride will not cause the Lord to give you a lesson in humility.

# WEEK 27
# PRAYER

DAY 1
SUGGESTED READING
MARK 11:24

> **²⁴ Therefore I tell you, whatever you ask for in prayer, believe that you have received it, and it will be yours. (NIV)**

God is willing and wanting to answer our prayers. He will answer them in a way that is best for us. He tells us that we must believe that he will answer our prayers for it to happen.

God answers our prayers because of his grace and mercy. Like our free gift of salvation through Jesus, answered prayers are also free. It is not by works but a grace. If we had to be sin free we would never have our prayers answered. He understands that we are not perfect that is why He tells for us to pray, "forgive us our sins". (Luke 11:4 NIV)

The bottom line is that we must have faith to have prayers answered. When we pray, we must believe that they will be answered and praise God for being there for us in our time of need.

*DAY 2*
*SUGGESTED READING*
*JEREMIAH 29:12*

## **¹² Then you will call on me and come and pray to me, and I will listen to you. (NIV)**

God tells us to come to him with our problems. He can only help us if we bring our concerns to him in prayer.

He tells us that he will listen. This is a promise that he cannot renege on. No matter how small or large the concern is God will listen. He will also answer our prayers in his own time. Be patient, when praying. God knows what we need and will address our concerns in the best way for us.

DAY 3
SUGGESTED READING
MATTHEW 6:6

> **⁶ But when you pray, go into your room, close the door and pray to your Father, who is unseen. Then your Father, who sees what is done in secret, will reward you. (NIV)**

It goes without saying that Christians pray. There is prayer for the public and there is prayer that is private. Public prayer is typically for the world and people in general. It can be in a smaller group asking for specific things.

This verse is obviously pertaining to the private prayer. When we are alone and in our most humble self, the Lord will be there with us. It is at this time when we are devoting all of what we are to the Lord. This is our most sincere state.

*DAY 4*
*SUGGESTED READING*
*JAMES 1:6*

**⁶ But when you ask, you must believe and not doubt, because the one who doubts is like a wave of the sea, blown and tossed by the wind. (NIV)**

Always ask the Lord when you have concerns or need direction. The Lord will answer. This is a promise of the Lord.

You must have faith though. If you doubt, then you are not trusting in the Lord. Prayer without faith will not be answered.

DAY 5
SUGGESTED READING
JAMES 5:13

**¹³ Is anyone among you in trouble? Let them pray.
Is anyone happy? Let them sing songs of praise.
(NIV)**

James speaks of two things in this verse. He mentions Pray and Praise. Both of these areas of Christian life are frequently lacking. Pray and Praise are not typically thought of whether there is trouble in our life or happiness.

Make a conscious effort to pray to the Lord when you are troubled. He tells us to bring our troubles to him. Rely on the Lord's mercy to see us through the challenging times in our life.

Also praise the Lord when things are doing good in our life. It is easy to forget to praise the Lord when our lives are relatively trouble free. We tend to not pray to the Lord in praise as we do in times of trouble. But in either case, Pray.

DAY 6
SUGGESTED READING
MATTHEW 6:7

**⁷And when you pray, do not keep on babbling like pagans, for they think they will be heard because of their many words. (NIV)**

In the early days, when God was trying to endure the Jews to him, he warned of prayer to other gods. In this case, the worshipers of Baal would pray from morning until noon using repetition in an attempt to get heard. There are religions today that do the same thing. To say things repeatedly loses the conviction behind the words and become vain.

Jesus encourages us to pray continuously. However, he tells us that are prayers should be heart felt. We need to consider what we are asking for and pray constantly for it. God knows what we want and is willing to receive our prayers. Why we pray continuously is to know in our soul that this is what we really desire. We also want God to know that we are completely dependent on him to answer our prayers.

DAY 7
SUGGESTED READING
MATTHEW 6:9 - 13

**⁹ After this manner therefore pray ye: Our Father which art in heaven, Hallowed be thy name.**

**¹⁰ Thy kingdom come, Thy will be done in earth, as it is in heaven.**

**¹¹ Give us this day our daily bread.**

**¹² And forgive us our debts, as we forgive our debtors.**

**¹³ And lead us not into temptation, but deliver us from evil: For thine is the kingdom, and the power, and the glory, for ever. Amen. (KJV)**

This is the prayer that Jesus taught his disciples. It is the perfect prayer because Jesus know exactly how to address God.

This prayer should be memorized and though it may not be used daily, it is a perfect template on how we should pray, giving reverence to God, giving praise and obtaining guidance.

# WEEK 28
# PREACHING

DAY 1
SUGGESTED READING
MARK 16:15

**¹⁵ He said to them, "Go into all the world and preach the gospel to all creation. (NIV)**

All of God's disciples are instructed to preach the gospel of Jesus. This is to the Jews and Gentiles. There is no distinction on the class of man. Salvation is for the rich or the poor. Race or gender is not a limiting. Jesus said, "to all man".

This holds today for the modern Christian. We should be ready to share the gospel of Jesus with all non-believers. In fact, it is our duty to preach the gospel. No matter where you are, at home or on vacation, in your town or in another country be ready to preach.

*DAY 2*
*SUGGESTED READING*
*EXODUS 4:10 - 12*

> [10] **Moses said to the LORD, "Pardon your servant, Lord. I have never been eloquent, neither in the past nor since you have spoken to your servant. I am slow of speech and tongue."**
>
> [11] **The LORD said to him, "Who gave human beings their mouths? Who makes them deaf or mute? Who gives them sight or makes them blind? Is it not I, the LORD?**
>
> [12] **Now go; I will help you speak and will teach you what to say." (NIV)**

Public speaking was difficult for Moses as it is for many of us. Though he was a philosopher, leader and statesman, oration was not in his skillset. This did not mean what he said wasn't powerful.

Don't worry about your weakness in oration. The Lord promises to help strengthen our words to get his message across. As we continue to preach the Word of God, with his help, experience with make it easier.

Start by speaking to small groups. Get comfortable with this and move to larger groups. The Lord will assist us if we pray for his assistance.

DAY 3
SUGGESTED READING
1 CORINTHIANS 2:13

**¹³ This is what we speak, not in words taught us by human wisdom but in words taught by the Spirit, explaining spiritual realities with Spirit-taught words. (NIV)**

Everyone has a way to preach. There are those who are born with an eloquent tongue and can preach to the masses. Then there are those who can only preach in small groups.

Regardless of how we preach, the gift is given to us by God. It is the Holy Spirit within us that helps us deliver his message and it is the Holy Spirit that moves those listening to receive the message of the gospel.

We are but a tool of God. He uses us as a conduit to deliver his Word. When the Holy Spirit is guiding our words, we can make understandable the wisdom of the Bible. Those who allow the Holy Spirit to teach them will understand what God is saying to them.

*DAY 4*
*SUGGESTED READING*
*1 CORINTHIANS 1:17*

**¹⁷ For Christ did not send me to baptize, but to preach the gospel—not with wisdom and eloquence, lest the cross of Christ be emptied of its power. (NIV)**

We, like Paul, are not sent to baptize unless we are pastors in the church. So normally we are sharing the gospel of Christ. We can preach in a small group or preach in front of an auditorium full of people.

The importance of our preaching is to bring people to the understanding of Jesus's mission on earth. We should be careful not to speak in such a way as to take away from the message of the crucifixion.

*DAY 5*
*SUGGESTED READING*
*2 TIMOTHY 4:2*

**² Preach the word; be prepared in season and out of season; correct, rebuke and encourage—with great patience and careful instruction. (NIV)**

If we are going to preach the word of God and the gospel of Jesus, we must be prepared to say things to people that they may not want to hear. Basically, "Preach the word; be instant in season, out of season; reprove, rebuke, exhort with all longsuffering and doctrine". (2 Timothy 4:2 KJV)

We must be ready to preach no matter when it is called upon us to do so. Sometimes the situation dictates when we need to teach the message of Christ.

*DAY 6*
*SUGGESTED READING*
*ACTS 10:42*

**⁴² He commanded us to preach to the people and to testify that he is the one whom God appointed as judge of the living and the dead. (NIV)**

The apostles are constantly talking about preaching the gospel of Jesus to the people of the world. This verse is the only reference to which Peter specific talks about Jesus being the judge of the living and the dead.

Jesus will judge all people on the last day who come before him from his seat of judgement on the right hand of God, the Father Almighty. Jesus explained this to the apostles and commands that we as believers today continue the message.

DAY 7
SUGGESTED READING
ACTS 8:4

**⁴ Therefore they that were scattered abroad went everywhere preaching the word. (KJV)**

The reason that we have the Word of God today is because of the persecution of the Christians in Jerusalem in the first century. The believers were scattered to escape persecution.

This did not diminish their faith and they preached the gospel of Jesus wherever they went. This has continued for over 2000 years and believers are still preaching the Word. This is not designated to only those trained to preach but to the common Christian who love Jesus and proclaim their believe in his mission here on Earth.

# WEEK 29
# RESURRECTION

DAY 1
SUGGESTED READING
JOHN 11:25 - 26

**²⁵ Jesus said to her, "I am the resurrection and the life. The one who believes in me will live, even though they die;**

**²⁶ and whoever lives by believing in me will never die. Do you believe this?" (NIV)**

Martha was told by Jesus that her brother will rise from death. She believes in this as she is a believer in Jesus being the Son of God. Jesus demonstrates that he is the master of death now and at the general resurrection.

These verses are the promise and the truth of Christ. The message pertains to our spiritual life not our physical one. We know that this is the principle reason that Christ came to Earth. His death for our sins must be believed if one is to attain the gift of life.

*DAY 2*
*SUGGESTED READING*
*MATTHEW 28:5 - 6*

**⁵ The angel said to the women, "Do not be afraid, for I know that you are looking for Jesus, who was crucified.**

**⁶ He is not here; he has risen, just as he said. Come and see the place where he lay. (NIV)**

Jesus spoke many times to his disciples regarding his resurrection, but they didn't appear to understand what he was trying to tell them. They were taken by surprise when they were told he was missing.

The religious leaders paid the Roman guards who were stationed to guard the tomb to say he was stolen. This was not the case as an angel appeared before Mary Magdalene, Mary the mother of James, and Salome who came to anoint his body with spices. "And entering the tomb, they saw a young man sitting on the right side, dressed in a white robe, and they were alarmed. And he said to them, "Do not be alarmed. You seek Jesus of Nazareth, who was crucified. He has risen; he is not here. See the place where they laid him. But go, tell his disciples and Peter that he is going before you to Galilee. There you will see him, just as he told you." (Mark 16:5 – 7 NIV)

DAY 3
SUGGESTED READING
1 CORINTHIANS 15:3 – 4

**³ For what I received I passed on to you as of first importance: that Christ died for our sins according to the Scriptures,**

**⁴ that he was buried, that he was raised on the third day according to the Scriptures, (NIV)**

Throughout the Bible we have been told of the coming of Jesus, the sacrifice of Jesus and the resurrection of Jesus. It was never stated in the past Scriptures that he would rise on the 3rd day, but it was implied.

It was prophesized by Moses, Isaac, Jonah, David and others in the Old Testament about the coming of Jesus. About his trials and tribulations. About him being the savior of man. Everything that was prophesized about him occurred during his life in the New Testament.

*DAY 4*
*SUGGESTED READING*
*LUKE 24:6 - 7*

**⁶ He is not here; he has risen! Remember how he told you, while he was still with you in Galilee:**

**⁷ 'The Son of Man must be delivered over to the hands of sinners, be crucified and on the third day be raised again.' (NIV)**

It is unfortunate that no one saw the resurrection of Jesus but to being told by God's Angels that this event occurred is amazing in itself. This event is the most important event in human history.

This is the purpose of Jesus being on Earth. This is the expression of God's true love for his children. The sacrifice that Jesus made assures our salvation.

St. Luke is not so sure initially. This is understandable. He is a physician and approaches things with a scientific eye. To have him accept this as a miracle after a thorough examination of the evidence is a testament of the authenticity of the power of Christ.

DAY 5
SUGGESTED READING
1CORINTHIANS 15:21

**²¹ For since by man came death, by man came also the resurrection of the dead. (KJV)**

In Genesis, Adam failed God and doomed all man to death. When Adam sinned he became mortal, and through him all became mortal. The one act of eating of the Tree of Knowledge not only brought death to man, but death to everything living on Earth.

As mortality came by the man Adam, immortality comes to us by the man Jesus Christ. To have sin removed and life restored is why resurrection is important. The resurrection is the assurance that all who believe in him will be saved and never have to suffer the eternal death that awaits the unbeliever.

DAY 6
SUGGESTED READING
LUKE 24:46 - 47

**⁴⁶ And said unto them, Thus it is written, and thus it behooved Christ to suffer, and to rise from the dead the third day:**

**⁴⁷ And that repentance and remission of sins should be preached in his name among all nations, beginning at Jerusalem. (KJV)**

The Old Testament repeatedly prophesized the coming of Christ. Though much inference it speaks of the resurrection of Christ and the importance of this event.

This being the most important event in the Bible, every Christian is charged preach the message of redemption through repentance and remission of sins. Christians began delivering this message after Christ died and continues until today. The importance of this message should continue until the return of Christ to Earth.

DAY 7
SUGGESTED READING
ROMANS 8:11

**¹¹ And if the Spirit of him who raised Jesus from the dead is living in you, he who raised Christ from the dead will also give life to your mortal bodies because of his Spirit who lives in you. (NIV)**

The resurrection is the most important fact of the gospel. God shows his love to all mankind by sending the Holy Spirit to save us as he did so for Jesus.

Excepting Christ gives us the gift of the resurrection which is eternal life. This gift is attained through faith that the gospel is true. If the resurrection of Jesus did not happen; "your faith is futile, and you are still in your sins". (1 Corinthians 15:17 NIV)

We as Christians believe in the resurrection of Christ. This is a promise of God that we rejoice in and praise God for. It is a fact that Christ rose from the dead. Therefore, it is a fact that those who believe in him will also be resurrected like him.

# WEEK 30
# SANCTIFICATION

## DAY 1
## SUGGESTED READING
## 2 THESSALONIANS 2:13

**¹³ But we ought always to give thanks to God for you, brothers beloved by the Lord, because God chose you as the first fruits to be saved, through sanctification by the Spirit and belief in the truth. (ESV)**

God gives all man the right to be saved. It is the choice of man that will bring him into Christ family. Unfortunately, broad is the road that leads to destruction and most will take it.

Give thanks that you have been chosen by God. You took the narrow path and chose to believe, and this has sanctified you to Him.

*DAY 2*
*SUGGESTED READING*
*JOHN 17:17*

## ¹⁷ Sanctify them through thy truth: thy word is truth. (KJV)

As Christians, we are set apart from others to share the truth of the Bible. This is told to us repeatedly by the apostles and by Jesus. Any doctrine that is taught not from the Bible is not the Word of God and is not profitable for teaching and not the truth.

To be Christian is to be sanctified by the truth of the Bible. Preaching this truth is the only way to save others.

*DAY 3*
*SUGGESTED READING*
*GALATIANS 2:20*

**[20] I am crucified with Christ: nevertheless, I live; yet not I, but Christ liveth in me: and the life which I now live in the flesh I live by the faith of the Son of God, who loved me, and gave himself for me. (KJV)**

When you are sanctified in Christ, you are a changed person. You are given the gift of the Holy Spirit to reside in you. This causes you to have different priorities as you shed your old sinful nature and assume the mantle of righteousness.

Praise God for the sacrifice of his Son who loved us and gave his life for us.

*DAY 4*
*SUGGESTED READING*
*1 CORINTHIANS 6:11*

**¹¹ And that is what some of you were. But you were washed, you were sanctified, you were justified in the name of the Lord Jesus Christ and by the Spirit of our God. (NIV)**

Though we are sinners, we are cleansed of our sins through Christ. This verse reminds us that we had been like those who continue to commit sin but aren't now.

Our salvation is an occurrence of three situations: our sins are washed away, our lives are justified through the suffering of Christ, our sanctification is from the Holy Spirit.

We do not earn this through works. We are saved by the grace of God through faith.

DAY 5
SUGGESTED READING
1 CORINTHIANS 12:13

**¹³ For we were all baptized by one Spirit so as to form one body—whether Jews or Gentiles, slave or free—and we were all given the one Spirit to drink. (NIV)**

Christ is the head of the body. We are the body. We become part of the body through the symbolic act of baptism. This baptism represents the cleansing and rebirth of our spiritual body.

The reality is that believing in Christ and accepting him as our savior allows the Holy Spirit to enter our body. This happens to all who accept Christ. This is the only Holy Spirit that exist and binds us all as Christians to the body of Christ.

*DAY 6*
*SUGGESTED READING*
*1 PETER 1:2*

**² who have been chosen according to the foreknowledge of God the Father, through the sanctifying work of the Spirit, to be obedient to Jesus Christ and sprinkled with his blood: Grace and peace be yours in abundance. (NIV)**

God choose us to preach his doctrine to all man. This was done in the beginning. The election is not accidental and each of us chosen fits into God's plan for the future.

To be sanctified by requires those chosen to accept the gospel of Christ and convert to a new, reborn person spiritually. Through sanctification, the spirit of the individual is empowered. There is an internal change of the heart and soul. The individual is now set apart as a chosen of God.

As we grow in the Holy Spirit, we will be rewarded for our service and obligations with happiness and posterity.

*DAY 7*
*SUGGESTED READING*
*1 PETER 1:13 - 16*

**¹³ Therefore, with minds that are alert and fully sober, set your hope on the grace to be brought to you when Jesus Christ is revealed at his coming.**

**¹⁴ As obedient children, do not conform to the evil desires you had when you lived in ignorance.**

**¹⁵ But just as he who called you is holy, so be holy in all you do;**

**¹⁶ for it is written: "Be holy, because I am holy." (NIV)**

Sanctification is God's will for us. To be sanctified is to be set apart for a special use. In religious terms, it is to be made holy.

As Christians we are to consider seriously our duty to God and man. There will be trials that will call us back to a sinful time which we must overcome. Guard you heart and mind against anything contrary to the nature of God. Satan will constantly tempt you. God will be there to help us through.

Being holy does not make us better than others. It does not give us power to judge. It is a way of life that we aspire to because this was the life of Christ. We were chosen by God for a unique purpose. The gifts he has endowed us with are to be used to complete the plan of God. In the end, when Jesus returns to judge both the living and the dead, we will be glorified with the promises from God for our obedience and faithfulness.

# WEEK 31
# SECOND COMING

DAY 1
SUGGESTED READING
HEBREWS 9:28

**²⁸ so Christ was sacrificed once to take away the sins of many; and he will appear a second time, not to bear sin, but to bring salvation to those who are waiting for him. (NIV)**

Every Christian gets excited about this promise of God. Jesus, as a man of no sin, was sacrificed to bear all the sins of man, from the beginning until judgement day. Upon his sacrifice he is then referred to in the Bible as Christ, the savior of man.

The principle concept of the Bible is resurrection. It was prophesized from the Old Testament and realized in the New Testament. Every Christian became a Christian because of their belief that there will be a "second coming" of Christ to collect his family to him. This is the salvation to eternal life. This is the highest attainment that man can reach.

Woe to those who don't accept the gospel of Christ, for they have nothing to live for in the end.

*DAY 2*
*SUGGESTED READING*
*MATTHEW 24:44*

## **⁴⁴ So you also must be ready, because the Son of Man will come at an hour when you do not expect him. (NIV)**

It has been said, "It is useless to set the day and hour for Christ's coming. It is folly to neglect it." Luke 21:36 warns us about the return of Christ and questions are we prepared.

The apostles questioned Jesus regarding the signs of his return and the end of the age. Jesus warns of false prophets that will claim that they know when he will return and will offer evidence to support their claims. Jesus tells them that no one, no man or angel, not even he knows when the date will be. Only God knows the date of his return.

The Bible gives us things to ponder regarding being prepared for his return:

- God told Noah that he was going to destroy the Earth. He told him what to do to prepare for this. Noah did tell others about God's plan but was not taken seriously. They were not prepared when the flood came and destroyed all but those in the ark.
- Matthew 24:40-41 speaks of the Rapture; Two men will be in the field; one will be taken and the other left. Two women will be grinding with a hand mill; one will be taken and the other left. (NIV)
- "Like a thief in the night". (1 Thessalonians 5:2 NIV) We lock our doors, install security systems and have guard dogs to prepare against theft. How prepared are we for Christ return?

The message is clear. Prepare for the return of Christ. Live righteously and love your fellow man.

DAY 3
SUGGESTED READING
TITUS 2:13

**¹³ while we wait for the blessed hope—the appearing of the glory of our great God and Savior, Jesus Christ, (NIV)**

Christ will return. This is a promise of the Bible. Christians know this and devote their lives to righteousness and wait in expectation of this momentous event.

While we wait, we must preach the message of the Bible to all who are not believers. We must do this while there is still time. Though he tells us that he will return, not even he does not know the date and time.

And this is why we continue the Lords work.

DAY 4
SUGGESTED READING
REVELATION 1:7

> **⁷ "Look, he is coming with the clouds,"**
> **and "every eye will see him,**
> **even those who pierced him";**
> **and all peoples on earth "will mourn because of him."**
> **So shall it be! Amen. (NIV)**

When Jesus first appeared, he came to make atonement for the sins of man. For his efforts, he was ridiculed, mocked and eventually crucified by those that he was trying to save.

When he appears the second time, everyone will see him. He will come in all his glory. In the clouds with angels and trumpeting and his light will uncover all darkness. Those who have not accepted him will suffer the judgement of God.

DAY 5
SUGGESTED READING
LUKE 21;34 - 36

**³⁴ "Be careful, or your hearts will be weighed down with carousing, drunkenness and the anxieties of life, and that day will close on you suddenly like a trap.**

**³⁵ For it will come on all those who live on the face of the whole earth.**

**³⁶ Be always on the watch, and pray that you may be able to escape all that is about to happen, and that you may be able to stand before the Son of Man." (NIV)**

It is easy to get caught up in the indulgences of the world. This is especially true for those who have achieved a certain level of posterity. It is also very easy to dwell on our anxieties regarding our life situation. It is in these times that we are thinking more of earthly things that ethereal things.

Keep the Laws of the Lord close to your heart that you will not break them. Acknowledge God in all that you do. Bring your problems to God in prayer. Living the righteous life will keep us prepared for the return of Christ.

*DAY 6*
*SUGGESTED READING*
*REVELATION 22:12*

## ¹² "Look, I am coming soon! My reward is with me, and I will give to each person according to what they have done. (NIV)

The purpose of the Second Coming to man is to pass judgement on their actions according to their works. The purpose of the Second Coming to Christians is the acceptance of the salvation that is the promise of the Bible.

Jesus says that he will bring his reward with him. However, this is a double-edged sword. The reward can be gracious, or it can be a curse. At the time of judgement, one's life will be examined, so shall their spirit. The standard by which they will be judged is the decisions that they have made with regard to the Word of God.

Jesus died once and ascended. He will return as Christ and will judge the living and the dead. The believers will rise from the grave and be publicly acknowledged as God's children. These and those believers alive will be rewarded with admittance into Heaven. The unbelievers will be rewarded with judgement. This judgement will be spiritual death, the complete separation from the presence of God forever. He will be prepared to make this judgement immediately.

*DAY 7*
*SUGGESTED READING*
*1 THESSALONIANS 4:16 - 17*

**¹⁶ For the Lord himself will come down from heaven, with a loud command, with the voice of the archangel and with the trumpet call of God, and the dead in Christ will rise first.**

**¹⁷ After that, we who are still alive and are left will be caught up together with them in the clouds to meet the Lord in the air. And so we will be with the Lord forever. (NIV)**

When Christ returns, he will come with all his glory and fanfare. He will call the dead to rise showing his command over life and death. He will then collect all his people and bring them with him in the clouds to reside with him forever.

This is the gracious reward of God to those who have believed in him and live the Christian life. These verses fulfill the promise of God to his people. Christians believe this with every fiber of their being and long for this "second coming".

# WEEK 32
# PATIENCE

DAY 1
SUGGESTED READING
PROVERBS 14:29

> **²⁹ Whoever is patient has great understanding, but one who is quick-tempered displays folly.**
> **(NIV)**

Controlling your spirit is basic to gaining wisdom. One who controls his spirit has a greater understanding of himself and of human nature in general. The patient person listens and considers before responding without thought.

Impatience is not a sin but surely can lead to it. Impatience leads to quick, thoughtless reaction rather than ordered thinking. It shows no control of oneself or emotions. Comments and actions made without thought will typically cause resentment or a bad outcome.

The Bible tells us that God is slow to anger. Anger is not a sin, but it must be controlled. It can lead to sin because the greater its intensity the less understanding is being utilized. So, this gives us an example of how to be patient.

Jesus was a very patient man. He had control of his emotions. When his enemies tried to provoke him to anger he always exercised reason as opposed to anger.

*DAY 2*
*SUGGESTEDD READING*
*PROVERBS 16:32*

**³² He who is slow to anger is better than the mighty,
and he who rules his spirit than he who takes a city. (MEV)**

Anger is rarely a helpful emotion. It is frequently used by the people in positions of power to exert their authority over their subordinates. Anger typically causes actions that are more severe than they need to be. It neglects counsel and causes one to say things that they later regret.

It takes more courage, discipline, strength and wisdom to control one's emotions, especially anger. These are the attributes of a patient person. The person who directs all their passion to good is more honorable person than the person who intimidates with anger. This person displays the qualities of Jesus who displayed patience in teaching his disciples or the non-believers.

DAY 3
SUGGESTED READING
PSALM 27:14

## ¹⁴ Wait for the LORD;
## be strong and take heart
## and wait for the LORD. (NIV)

We have many real problems that we have no answers for. The non-believer will try and solve their problems using the means of man. They may have success, or they may not. There is no guarantee.

Christians have the same problems. The difference is that we have God. He tells us to, "Seek his face". (Psalms 105:4 KJV) The Lord wants us to bring our problems to him. He does not quantify this. All problems can be taken to him. The Lord will answer our prayers. He knows what we need and what the future holds so we need to be patient and wait for his response. Our prays will be answered in accordance to the will of God.

*DAY 4*
*SUGGESTED READING*
*EXODUS 14:14*

## ¹⁴ The LORD will fight for you; you need only to be still." (NIV)

In times of our greatest difficulties we need to keep our faith and trust in the Lord to fight for us. Always acknowledge him and do not trust our own means.

The hard part for us is that we want our prayers answered immediately. We are impatient beings and constantly seek instant gratification. We must be patient when it comes to the Lord answering our prayers. He will do so, but in his own time.

DAY 5
SUGGESTED READING
1 TIMOTHY 1:16

**¹⁶ But for that very reason I was shown mercy so that in me, the worst of sinners, Christ Jesus might display his immense patience as an example for those who would believe in him and receive eternal life. (NIV)**

Paul, in another life, spent his time prosecuting Christians. He felt that he must be the worst of the sinners. Yet, he was saved by Jesus and became one of his greatest apostles.

Jesus showed great patience with Paul as he does with all sinners. He does not punish sinners but spends time with them to make sure that they understand the message of the gospel.

We too must be patient with those seeking knowledge of the Word of God. Invest the time with them to get them to understand. You never know who the next Paul will be.

*DAY 6*
*SUGGESTED READING*
*2 PETER 3:9*

**⁹ The Lord is not slow in keeping his promise, as some understand slowness. Instead he is patient with you, not wanting anyone to perish, but everyone to come to repentance. (NIV)**

This verse shows the patience of God. He wants everyone to have a chance to be saved. For this reason, he is willing to wait as long as possible.

What was not understood by the people of that time was how God views time. It is said that God views 1000 years as if it were 1 day. We understand that today but believers in the early days of Christianity thought that Jesus would return in their lifetime. Because he did not return, people started to leave the Church.

The lesson is not to be impatient for the return of Christ. Keep faithful and follow the Law of the Lord. No one, not even Christ, knows when the day of judgement is to occur. Only God knows the day.

DAY 7
SUGGESTED READING
ROMANS 8:24 - 25

**²⁴ For in this hope we were saved. But hope that is seen is no hope at all. Who hopes for what they already have? ²⁵ But if we hope for what we do not yet have, we wait for it patiently. (NIV)**

According to Wikipedia, Hope is an optimistic state of mind that is based on an expectation of positive outcomes with respect to events and circumstances in one's life or the world at ltarge.

Christians feel this way regarding their life. Christians view life positively because they have the promises of God from the Bible. But ultimately, Christians wait patiently for the Second Coming. They do this with steady perseverance and diligence to the Law of the Lord. It is this event that salvation is promised and what all Christians hope for.

# WEEK 33
# WISDOM

DAY 1
SUGGESTED READING
PROVERBS 3:13 - 18

¹³ Blessed are those who find wisdom,
those who gain understanding,
¹⁴ for she is more profitable than silver
and yields better returns than gold.
¹⁵ She is more precious than rubies;
nothing you desire can compare with her.
¹⁶ Long life is in her right hand;
in her left hand are riches and honor.
¹⁷ Her ways are pleasant ways,
and all her paths are peace.
¹⁸ She is a tree of life to those who take hold of her;
those who hold her fast will be blessed. (NIV)

There is nothing more valuable for Christians than the wisdom of the Word of God. It is represented by Christ who is Wisdom. Don't be fooled into thinking that anything earthly can compare to this wisdom as it leads to salvation.

*DAY 2*
*SUGGESTED READING*
*JAMES 1:5*

**⁵ If any of you lacks wisdom, you should ask God, who gives generously to all without finding fault, and it will be given to you. (NIV)**

Throughout the history of man, believers have questioned their knowledge. This was in reference to their ability to lead, their academic training, their knowledge of the Law of the Lord or ways of the world. The great leaders of man, Moses and David were concerned about their knowledge and abilities.

We can attain all that we need to know through study of the Bible and asking for understanding through prayer. God promises to give us wisdom. Don't rely on the word of others because they may not have sought God's help for understanding. People say many things with conviction that are just false. They may even believe what they are saying is true because they heard it said from that ubiquitous "They". How many times have we heard, "they say"? Only trust the Lord for wisdom or someone that has proven his knowledge of the Word of God.

DAY 3
SUGGESTED READING
PROVERBS 1:7

> **⁷ The fear of the LORD is the beginning of knowledge,
> but fools despise wisdom and instruction. (NIV)**

Wisdom begins with the fear of God. This fear is reverence for all that God represents. Without the foundation of God there is no base on which to start understanding the judgement to come and the grace of salvation.

Unbelievers do not live their lives according to the Bible and the Law of the Lord. Instead of devoting time to learn wisdom from the Bible, they spend their time on earthly pursuits.

Do not be jealous or envious of the apparent success of these servants of sin. Earthly possessions will mean nothing if one is ignorant of the Lord's Word.

*DAY 4*
*SUGGESTED READING*
*EPHESIANS 1:16 - 19*

**[16] I have not stopped giving thanks for you, remembering you in my prayers.**

**[17] I keep asking that the God of our Lord Jesus Christ, the glorious Father, may give you the Spirit of wisdom and revelation, so that you may know him better.**

**[18] I pray that the eyes of your heart may be enlightened in order that you may know the hope to which he has called you, the riches of his glorious inheritance in his holy people,**

**[19] and his incomparably great power for us who believe. That power is the same as the mighty strength. (NIV)**

Paul reminds us to remember others in prayer. He knows that wisdom comes from Jesus and ask that Jesus will impart this wisdom that the ones being prayed for will come to know him.

The message of Jesus is the most important knowledge that someone can attain. Without it one will never know God's love and mercy. With it all of God's promises are relevant.

DAY 5
SUGGESTED READING
PROVERBS 3:5

**⁵ Trust in the LORD with all your heart
and lean not on your own understanding; (NIV)**

There are times that we cannot solve problems in our life. We try to solve them, but the solutions typically fail. This is a choice of ours, relying on our pride to overcome adversity. He who trust in his own designs is a fool in God's eyes.

The Lord wants us to trust Him with not only our problems but in all aspects of our life. We can't possibly know what is in God's plan for us. We are working with limited understanding of the big picture. The Lord knows all, and His thoughts are divine, so he is in better position to address our problems and concerns

We must trust that God will take care of us as Christians even though we have no comprehension of the outcome of a situation. We must have faith that God knows what is best for us and will never fail us in our time of need.

*DAY 6*
*SUGGESTED READING*
*1 CORINTHIANS 1:30*

**³⁰ It is because of him that you are in Christ Jesus, who has become for us wisdom from God—that is, our righteousness, holiness and redemption. (NIV)**

It is through grace that we are saved. This is accepting Christ in us. We are reminded that no matter how much we want to be acknowledged for the material accomplishments, none can boast that they have greater favor from God.

Jesus Christ is our wisdom from God. His gospel is explained throughout the New Testament. His disciples record his sermons, his speeches, his parables, his miracles, his wisdom and his counsel.

Christ is the source of true spiritual wisdom. Christ is also the source of our spiritual gifts. Because these are given by grace, be humble and accept these gifts with supplication and thanks.

*DAY 7*
*SUGGESTED READING*
*2 TIMOTHY 3:16 - 17*

**[16] All Scripture is God-breathed and is useful for teaching, rebuking, correcting and training in righteousness,**

**[17] so that the servant of God may be thoroughly equipped for every good work. (NIV)**

To the non-believer the first verse may feel like any other self-help book. Most non-believers own one, but it sits on the shelf with the other self-help books not used. They own a Bible as if it is a talisman against evil.

To the believer this verse is the absolute vindication of the Bible as a source for all the wisdom a Christian need. The Bible is inspired by God. The Greek translation of this is "breathed out of the mouth of God". The Bible is the way God communicates with us in terms of instruction, wisdom and teaching.

The Bible is beneficial to both believers and non-believers. If studied diligently, it will prove to be reliable for every aspect of one's life. Every life situation can be addressed.

To the Christian, the Bible enhances our life's work. Seeking the wisdom of the Bible is not a chore but an activity that is enjoyed and satisfying. It is the one source that can be relied upon without reservation of correctness.

# WEEK 34 WORKS

DAY 1
SUGGESTED READING
MATTHEW 5:16

**¹⁶ In the same way, let your light shine before others, that they may see your good deeds and glorify your Father in heaven. (NIV)**

In all ways, through conversation, through presentation and through good works, let man see that you are a child of God.

It doesn't matter what one thinks of you for your behavior is to glorify God. Always let it be seen that you are a good Christian. It is your inner being that radiates the true message of the gospel that may lead the non-believer to seek further knowledge. Let them see the power of righteousness shining through you.

DAY 2
SUGGESTED READING
JAMES 2:14 - 17

**¹⁴ What good is it, my brothers and sisters, if someone claims to have faith but has no deeds? Can such faith save them?**

**¹⁵ Suppose a brother or a sister is without clothes and daily food.**

**¹⁶ If one of you says to them, "Go in peace; keep warm and well fed," but does nothing about their physical needs, what good is it?**

**¹⁷ In the same way, faith by itself, if it is not accompanied by action, is dead. (NIV)**

James presents a conundrum in his discussion of faith and works. In James 2:24 he states, "You see that a person is considered righteous by what they do and not by faith alone". (NIV) Paul in his letter to the Romans stated, "A person is justified not by the works of the law but through faith in Jesus Christ". (Galatians 2:16 NIV)

Though this has caused much debate, I think that James actually believes that we can be righteous through faith. James believes that faith begins with the Word of God that gives us life. Once one accepts the Word of God as true and accepts Christ as savior, the Holy Spirit changes them to want to do good works and to pass the message of the gospel on to others.

DAY 3
SUGGESTED READING
HEBREWS 13:16

**[16] And do not forget to do good and to share with others, for with such sacrifices God is pleased. (NIV)**

It is easy to forget benevolence. We are reminded to remember to share with others. This is especially pertinent to the poor. It also pertains to our enemies.

What God has given us we should share when we can. We don't do this for profit. We don't do this to gain position in their eyes. We do this out of love for our fellow man. This is the mindset that we must develop. The sacrifices we make are not unnoticed by God

DAY 4
SUGGESTED READING
GALATIANS 6:9

**⁹ Let us not become weary in doing good, for at the proper time we will reap a harvest if we do not give up. (NIV)**

Doing the work of God is difficult. I constantly am reminded of the verses:

- Enter through the narrow gate. For wide is the gate and broad is the road that leads to destruction, and many enter through it.
- But small is the gate and narrow the road that leads to life, and only a few find it. (Matthew 7:13 – 14 NIV)

Few people are interested in what you have to say or want to argue agnostic or atheistic views.

We must exercise patience and be persistent in our message of faith and belief that our efforts will be rewarded in heaven. It is easy to give up and doubt our ability to convey the message of Christ, but like Moses who worried that he could not deliver the message of God, God will guide us and bolster our spirits to continue.

DAY 5
SUGGESTED READING
TITUS 2:7

**⁷ In everything set them an example by doing what is good. In your teaching show integrity, seriousness (NIV)**

Whether preaching or teaching the gospel of Christ, it is important to present oneself in a professional manner. Present the gospel in a way that your audience sees the grace of God upon you. Speak with conviction, being an example of how the Lord expects us to represent him.

DAY 6
SUGGESTED READING
1 PETER 3:13 - 17

**¹³ Who is going to harm you if you are eager to do good?**

**¹⁴ But even if you should suffer for what is right, you are blessed. "Do not fear their threats; do not be frightened."**

**¹⁵ But in your hearts revere Christ as Lord. Always be prepared to give an answer to everyone who asks you to give the reason for the hope that you have. But do this with gentleness and respect,**

**¹⁶ keeping a clear conscience, so that those who speak maliciously against your good behavior in Christ may be ashamed of their slander.**

**¹⁷ For it is better, if it is God's will, to suffer for doing good than for doing evil. (NIV)**

The Christian life is difficult because we are persecuted for our love for Christ. We live a strict lifestyle that we are committed which is hard to understand for the unbeliever. As a result, the Christian life is suffering. Always believe that suffering for good is better than suffering for sin. In the end there is vindication for what is endured.

Revisit the Beatitude:

- Blessed are those who have been persecuted for righteousness' sake, for theirs is the Kingdom of Heaven.

- Blessed are you when people reproach you, persecute you, and say all kinds of evil against you falsely, for my sake.
- Rejoice, and be exceedingly glad, for great is your reward in heaven. For that is how they persecuted the prophets who were before you" (Matthew 5:10-12 ASV).

*DAY 7*
*SUGGESTED READING*
*1 CORINTHIANS 15:58*

**⁵⁸ Therefore, my dear brothers and sisters, stand firm. Let nothing move you. Always give yourselves fully to the work of the Lord, because you know that your labor in the Lord is not in vain. (NIV)**

The day of resurrection is coming. Only God knows the day. Not even Jesus knows, so we are to be ready. We must persevere and not be moved from the ministry that is the work of the Lord.

It is not easy to stay committed to preaching the Word of God in the presence of a sinful world that is quick to criticize and persecute. Pray for strength constantly to keep your spirit strong in the face of adversary. Pray for those who are having difficulty staying committed to the Lord's work.

Persistence in preaching the gospel will eventually produce fruit. The more someone is exposed to the Word of God, the more its message will start penetrating their hardened heart to the light of Jesus. Stay steadfast

# WEEK 35
# WORLDLINESS

DAY 1
SUGGESTED READING
1 JOHN 2:15 - 17

**¹⁵ Do not love the world or anything in the world. If anyone loves the world, love for the Father is not in them.**

**¹⁶ For everything in the world—the lust of the flesh, the lust of the eyes, and the pride of life—comes not from the Father but from the world.**

**¹⁷ The world and its desires pass away, but whoever does the will of God lives forever. (NIV)**

Everything in the world was put here by God. Therefore, all is put here for the glorification of God. However, Satin twist things in a way as to turn them to be used in a sinful nature.

Christians must be wary of the allure to corruption and avoid the thoughts and activities that can lead us away from God. The more one leans towards sinful behavior, the farther away from God one strays.

Keep focused on the Law of the Lord. Pray for strength and guidance to keep in the ways of righteousness.

*DAY 2*
*SUGGESTED READING*
*MATTHEW 6:24*

**²⁴ "No one can serve two masters. Either you will hate the one and love the other, or you will be devoted to the one and despise the other. You cannot serve both God and money. (NIV)**

Jesus explains that it is not possible to equally serve two masters. One will command more dedication than the other. Eventually, preference will be directed toward the one that we commit to emotionally and spiritually. If you seek the comforts and gifts of the world, then you do not seek the gifts of God. The temptation of what is attainable on Earth is difficult for many to resist, albeit temporary. Gifts from God, unlike gifts from the Earth, will never fade away in time.

Our choices, as Christians, are to be a servant to God or be a servant to Satan. Being Christians, we have already made the decision who we want to be our master. This doesn't mean that we will not be tempted to worldly desires. When faced with questionable decisions to make, think whether your decision is in compliance with the nature of God.

*DAY 3*
*SUGGESTED READING*
*ROMANS 12:2*

**² Do not conform to the pattern of this world but be transformed by the renewing of your mind. Then you will be able to test and approve what God's will is—his good, pleasing and perfect will. (NIV)**

The world offers many comforts and riches to be attained. Most people dedicate enormous amounts of energy to attain these things. The effort put into this detracts from seeking God. That is exactly what Satan wants to happen. He tempts us with things that will demand our focus, while spiritually we wither.

Accept Jesus and transform into a new being spiritually. This transformation exposes us to the will of God and changes us internally to realize that the gifts of the world are passing and do not provide real happiness.

*DAY 4*
*SUGGESTED READING*
*ROMANS 8:5*

**⁵ Those who live according to the flesh have their minds set on what the flesh desires; but those who live in accordance with the Spirit have their minds set on what the Spirit desires. (NIV)**

There is a distinction between the sinner and the righteous. The sinner focuses their life on the attainment of worldly possessions and worldly ways. They have no interest in what they cannot see. Their faith is in the possessions they have collected, the wealth they have accumulated and the power and status they have attained in the eyes of man.

The righteous has given their life to the service of God. Because of their belief and their faith, they do not worry about the things of the world. They know that God will provide for them the things that they need while doing His work. More important to them is the gifts given from the Lord and the promise of salvation.

Being reborn of the spirit redeems us from the desires of the flesh. One is now spiritually minded and seeks things to strengthen the spirit. They no longer live the worldly life but live because the spirit of Christ lives in them. This spirit seeks what is eternal not what is worldly.

*DAY 5*
*SUGGESTED READING*
*2 CORINTHINAS 1:12*

**¹² Now this is our boast: Our conscience testifies that we have conducted ourselves in the world, and especially in our relations with you, with integrity and godly sincerity. We have done so, relying not on worldly wisdom but on God's grace. (NIV)**

By nature, people try to do whatever seems the best for them. Their wisdom comes from worldly knowledge and experience. This is taught to them from childhood. Educational systems are developed to teach everyone the knowledge of the world and how to navigate through it with the least difficulty.

The knowledge obtained this way is earthly, unspiritual and demonic. For the world, this is sound advice. Ultimately, there is no spiritual gain and all that is acquired from the worldly knowledge will pass away.

The knowledge that is imparted to all of us throughout our life is not all bad. God put this knowledge here for us to uses. What is important for Christians though, is to put everything in perspective. We must use this knowledge in a way that does not compromise our faith and Christian life.

Like Paul, we must keep our relationship with God intact, acknowledging Him and praising Him in all that we do. We must always remember that he is our master not the world. To man, we must always be honest and straightforward. We must present ourselves with the utmost integrity so there is no question of our intention.

DAY 6
SUGGESTED READING
2 CORINTHIANS 1:17

> **¹⁷ Was I fickle when I intended to do this? Or do I make my plans in a worldly manner so that in the same breath I say both "Yes, yes" and "No, no"? (NIV)**

How often do we see and hear this happen? People are always promising to do something and not do it. On a larger scale, the world does the same thing. We are constantly promised happiness with pleasures, materialism and instant gratification. These promises lead to sin, and sin ultimately leads to unhappiness.

God can never be misconstrued in his speech or actions. God is either yes or no. There is no maybe in anything that God does. When Jesus came to the world he told us that he came to deliver the truth of God. We to should strive to do the same. We should say yes or no and not waver. We should always speak the truth.

DAY 7
SUGGESTED READING
TITUS 2:12

**¹² It teaches us to say "No" to ungodliness and worldly passions, and to live self-controlled, upright and godly lives in this present age, (NIV)**

In the letter to Titus from Paul, he explains the meaning of grace. Grace not only teaches us about salvation, but it also teaches us that we must say no to certain things.

Worldly desires oppose the will of God. The world will tempt us with desires of power, vanity, pleasure and material possessions. It is difficult to refuse any of these because life in the world is hard from the perspective of man. Succumbing to these desires will lead to sin and our undoing. No matter what we attain, desire cannot be fulfilled.

Grace teaches us to deny the desires of the world. It teaches us our duty to God. We must look to God in Christ for the strength to eliminate the desires of the world. The Holy Spirit will give us strength when faced with the temptation. We are redeemed of sin and cleansed in the eyes of God. Prayer and acknowledgement of God in all that we do will keep us in touch with the glories of the next world and not of this one.

# WEEK 36
# TAMING THE TONGUE

## DAY 1
## SUGGESTED READING
## PSALM 39:1

> **¹ I said, "I will watch my ways
> and keep my tongue from sin;
> I will put a muzzle on my mouth
> while in the presence of the wicked." (NIV)**

There is a time to speak and a time to be silent. This is a hard lesson to be learned. When we think evil thoughts, we should suppress them. Evil thoughts are full of emotions that can lead us to sin.

Especially in the presence of enemies, we need to be very careful about what we say. They do not have our best interest at heart. They are listening to every word that we say to use them to our disadvantage.

*DAY 2*
*SUGGESTED READING*
*PROVERBS 10:19*

**¹⁹ Sin is not ended by multiplying words,
but the prudent hold their tongues. (NIV)**

Talking to much will typically end up bad. When rambling on without giving thought to what is being said a point will weaken in strength. Further, truth is at risk as elaboration seems to equal exaggeration.

Think about what you want to say and keep it succinct and concise. This will keep one from the sin of slander.

*DAY 3*
*SUGGESTED READING*
*Matthew 15:11*

**¹¹ Not that which goeth into the mouth defileth a man; but that which cometh out of the mouth, this defileth a man. (KJV)**

The Pharisees believed that it was a sin to eat without washing your hands. They felt that sin enters through defiled food. This was based on traditions started in the Old Testament by the elders. They charged the disciples of Christ as being sinners because they didn't honor these traditions.

This verse is Christ counter to the accusation of the Pharisees. First, it is not a Law of the Lord to wash one's hands before eating. Food is not being defiled and causing sin to enter the body. What defiles man is the nature of his being. What proceeds out of his mouth will be sinful or corrupt.

DAY 4
SUGGESTED READING
JAMES 3:9 - 10

**With the tongue we praise our Lord and Father, and with it we curse men, who have been made in God's likeness. Out of the same mouth come praise and cursing. My brothers, this should not be. (NIV)**

This behavior is seen frequently amongst believers and unbelievers alike. James points this out. It is wrong to praise God then curse man. Who are we to judge someone else? This is not our place.

The saying that is appropriate here is, "if you have nothing to say nice about someone, don't say anything at all". By all means praise God but leave judgement to God. Speaking ill of someone is behavior that does not portray the image of Christ.

DAY 5
SUGGESTED READING
PROVERBS 18:21

**²¹ The tongue has the power of life and death, and those who love it will eat its fruit. (NIV)**

Words are powerful and can help or hurt someone. We always need to be aware of how we are using words because we never want to cause irreparable damage to someone who cares about what we say.

Words to a child can set that person on the right path or lead them to a life of distrust and confusion. Words to a teenager can give them proper direction or breed resentment and want of rebellion. Words to an adult can encourage them to a righteous life or lead them to sinful ways.

We must make sure what we are saying is always encouraging and consistent with Christ commandment to love our fellow man. Pray that God will direct the Holy Spirit to give us the gift of a loving nature and helpful tongue.

DAY 6
SUGGESTED READING
1 PETER 3:10

**¹⁰ For, "Whoever would love life
and see good days
must keep their tongue from evil
and their lips from deceitful speech. (NIV)**

This verse pertains to today and the future. The reward for controlling the tongue is knowing that sin is being avoided by your words. Always pray for strength in the spirit to help control impulse speech.

Controlling what you say is difficult especially when in disagreement with others. No one is always in agreement with someone else and one likes to believe their point of view is the correct one. Debate is healthy and not sinful but getting emotional about a point of view can lead to abusive and hurtful language. This is sinful and contrary to Gods will. It is also contrary to the behavior of Jesus.

DAY 7
SUGGESTED READING
JAMES 1:26

**²⁶ Those who consider themselves religious and yet do not keep a tight rein on their tongues deceive themselves, and their religion is worthless. (NIV)**

The character of man is developed by many things. Religion is heavily influential. Religion produces a certain behavior that is typical seen outward to all. One believes themselves religious by the way they act and express themselves.

If someone seems religious but says things contrary to the teachings of Jesus, then his religion is worthless. The religious person should not tell lies. The religious person should not gossip. The religious person should not swear. The religious person does not deceive.

Jesus clarifies the destructive nature of the tongue; "the things that come out of the mouth come from the heart, and these things defile a man" (Matthew 15:18 NIV).

# WEEK 37
# SUFFERING AND PRESECUTION

DAY 1
SUGGESTED READING
2 CORINTHIANS 1:3 - 4

**³ Praise be to the God and Father of our Lord Jesus Christ, the Father of compassion and the God of all comfort,**

**⁴ who comforts us in all our troubles, so that we can comfort those in any trouble with the comfort we ourselves receive from God. (NIV)**

Comfort comes from God. Jesus tells us that, "Let not your heart be troubled". (John 14:1 KJV) Life is hard for Christians and non-Christians alike and can seem insurmountable. The Christian has the Lord to pray to for help and comfort.

God can help in the worst of times and liven our souls. We must not be selfish in this blessing of the Lord and try to comfort the less fortunate. This is what Jesus did and what he told his disciples to do.

*DAY 2*
*SUGGESTED READING*
*ROMANS 5:3 - 4*

**³ Not only so, but we also glory in our sufferings, because we know that suffering produces perseverance;**

**⁴ perseverance, character; and character, hope. (NIV)**

Suffering comes in many forms. No one enjoys it. It breeds doubt and weakening of faith. In this state, it is hard to continue to call on God for help. The world will offer solutions that seem to be easier than waiting on Lord for relief.

Paul reminds us that we must persevere. This builds character and hope. We must remember that deliverance from our suffering is by the will of God. When we get through these trials, give praise to God for delivering us from our difficult times. We become stronger as a result.

DAY 3
SUGGESTED READING
PSALM 34:19

**¹⁹ Many are the afflictions of the righteous: but the LORD delivereth him out of them all. (KJV)**

Paul reminds Timothy that, "Indeed, all who desire to live a godly life in Christ Jesus will be persecuted" (2 Timothy 3:12 ESV). This message is pertinent to Christians of all ages. It is especially fitting today in a world that is relying on science more that the message of Jesus.

More and more Christians are persecuted worldwide and even killed for their Christianity. Fortunately, that is the extreme. In most cases, persecution is typically a condemnation of their belief.

Professing to be Christian is taking a chance at being persecuted in some form or the other. We should expect this. However, we should never try to hide our belief and pray for those who do not understand. In the end, The Lord will deliver us from this persecution.

*DAY 4*
*SUGGESTED READING*
*ROMANS 8:18*

**¹⁸ For I reckon that the sufferings of this present time are not worthy to be compared with the glory which shall be revealed in us. (KJV)**

Christians will suffer for their beliefs. It may be obvious with open distain or subtle where certain things are withheld like promotions at work or even getting a job. Christians are also persecuted by other religions that claim to be Christian.

Persecution is so common that todays Christian should waste time with whether they are being subject to it or not. Just know that God knows our suffering and we will be rewarded for our perseverance.

DAY 5
SUGGESTED READING
1 PETER 3:14

**¹⁴ But even if you should suffer for what is right, you are blessed. "Do not fear their threats; do not be frightened." (NIV)**

When suffering and persecution occurs be thankful that you are paying the price for being right. Though it may be hard stay focused on the Lord and you will have the strength to persevere.

Give praise to God to allow you the chance to show your faith in the presence of unbelievers. Be happy, not afraid or worried for the Lord is with you.

*DAY 6*
*SUGGESTED READING*
*ISAIAH 53:3 - 4*

> **³ He was despised and rejected by mankind,**
> **a man of suffering, and familiar with pain.**
> **Like one from whom people hide their faces**
> **he was despised, and we held him in low esteem.**
>
> **⁴ Surely, he took up our pain**
> **and bore our suffering,**
> **yet we considered him punished by God,**
> **stricken by him, and afflicted. (NIV)**

This is the most accurate prophesy of the coming of Jesus Christ from the Old Testament. It describes how he is viewed by man. It describes the suffering he is to bear.

This also describes the same path for Christians. The difference is that Christians can turn to Christ for relief. He has taken the suffering of all that one can come to him for salvation and know God's love.

DAY 7
SUGGESTED READING
JOB 1:20 - 21

**²⁰ At this, Job got up and tore his robe and shaved his head. Then he fell to the ground in worship**

**²¹ and said:**

**"Naked I came from my mother's womb, and naked I will depart. The LORD gave, and the LORD has taken away; may the name of the LORD be praised." (NIV)**

Job is the greatest example of a person who suffered for his faith. Every type of grief he had to endure, from loss of property to loss of family. Job had always been a religious man but as we learned this does not protect us from sorrow. His sorrow got so great that he wanted to die.

He did not blame God, he blamed himself for sin and believed that whatever was taken from him was done out of the righteousness of God.

The parable of Job is a testament to the blessings from God for perseverance through adversity. Like Job, Jesus suffered at the hands of the very people he was trying to save. Unlike Job, Jesus eventually died for his perseverance. The lesson to us is to live like both these men. Let adversity bring us closer to God. Stay faithful to God no matter what we have to endure for in the end we will be rewarded.

# WEEK 38
# NATURAL DISASTERS

DAY 1
SUGGESTED READING
ISAIAH 45:7

**⁷ I form the light and create darkness,
I bring prosperity and create disaster;
I, the LORD, do all these things. (NIV)**

God is emphatic about his sovereignty over the universe. Whether things are good or bad God is in control. Nothing occurs in the history of the world without his permission.

The verse should cause concern for the non-believer but comfort to the believer. Christians see disaster as part of the signs of the return of the Lord.

DAY 2
SUGGESTED READING
LUKE 21:11

**¹¹ There will be great earthquakes, famines and pestilences in various places, and fearful events and great signs from heaven. (NIV)**

Christ tells us what to look for as to the build up before he returns. The frequency of which these events will be on the rise. These are signs from Heaven.

Those who do not heed these events do not realize that the word of Christ is without fault and miss the message of Christianity. As these events continue to rise, we must use these events, supported by the biblical text, to spread the gospel of Christ.

*DAY 3*
*SUGGESTED READING*
*2 CHRONICLES 7:13 – 14*

**[13] "When I shut up the heavens so that there is no rain, or command locusts to devour the land or send a plague among my people,**

**[14] if my people, who are called by my name, will humble themselves and pray and seek my face and turn from their wicked ways, then I will hear from heaven, and I will forgive their sin and will heal their land. (NIV)**

This message, though given to the people of Israel, is for the people of the world. Nonetheless, humbling oneself and seeking God will reciprocate the effort in return. God wants to be attentive his people.

DAY 4
SUGGESTED READING
ZEPHANIAH 1:2 - 3

> ² **"I will sweep away everything
> from the face of the earth,"
> declares the LORD.**
> ³ **"I will sweep away both man and beast;
> I will sweep away the birds in the sky
> and the fish in the sea—
> and the idols that cause the wicked to stumble."**
>
> **"When I destroy all mankind
> on the face of the earth,"
> declares the LORD, (NIV)**

This message is for those who are in Christ. Christians know that there will be a second coming and that only those who chose to believe and be faithful will be protected by the Lord.

It is also a reminder that this has happened before in the case of Noah and Sodom and Gomorrah.

These are alarming times. As we become more technically advanced and scientifically inclined, we rely less and less on God. What is more important are the manmade idols money and power. The gifts of man are passing but perseverance in the Law of the Lord will save.

DAY 5
SUGGESTED READING
MARK 13:7 - 8

**⁷ When you hear of wars and rumors of wars, do not be alarmed. Such things must happen, but the end is still to come.**

**⁸ Nation will rise against nation, and kingdom against kingdom. There will be earthquakes in various places, and famines. These are the beginning of birth pains. (NIV)**

Jesus tells his disciples of the times that are to come. We also must take heed what he is saying. In the world today, these situations are all over the world. We are constantly hearing of the constant waring. Many we don't even understand the reasoning for them.

We also are hearing of increased disasters around the world. Fires, earthquakes, tsunamis, famine, all are signs of the coming of the Lord.

Be prepared. Keep faithful and stay righteous. Spread the gospel to those who are ignorant of the Word or lukewarm in their faith.

DAY 6
SUGGESTED READING
2 CHRONICLES 7:13 – 14

¹³ "When I shut up the heavens so that there is no rain, or command locusts to devour the land or send a plague among my people,

¹⁴ if my people, who are called by my name, will humble themselves and pray and seek my face and turn from their wicked ways, then I will hear from heaven, and I will forgive their sin and will heal their land. (NIV)

The Lord commands every natural event that occurs in the world. Whether is natural disaster or plague and pestilence. He has allowed these events over the course of history to make a point or to punish.

God wants us to turn from sin and acknowledge the righteousness. Not only on a personal level but on a national level. The Lord will hear the prayers of repentance from those who have humbled themselves and want change. He promises forgiveness.

DAY 7
SUGGESTED READING
Luke 21:11

**¹¹ There will be great earthquakes, famines and pestilences in various places, and fearful events and great signs from heaven. (NIV)**

As the time for the return of Christ approaches, more and frequent will the disasters occur. These visible signs should be recognized by all Christians for we are being told throughout the Bible of the end of times.

The unbeliever wants to blame these events on manmade involvement with the environment. This may be true to some degree but make no mistake, man's involvement in these occurrences is minute as opposed to the will of God.

# WEEK 39
# MANAGING TIME

*DAY 1*
*SUGGESTED READING*
*EPHESIANS 5:15 - 17*

**¹⁵ Be very careful, then, how you live—not as unwise but as wise,**

**¹⁶ making the most of every opportunity, because the days are evil.**

**¹⁷ Therefore do not be foolish but understand what the Lord's will is. (NIV)**

The Christian needs to be aware of how they appear before man. They must look at their inward self and outward self. Both aspects of self are developed through study of the Word of God. This is where wisdom is attained, and time is best used.

The unbeliever spends much of his time in activities that do nothing for spiritual growth. This is exactly what Satan wants. Diversion is rampart throughout the world and designed to waste our time.

*DAY 2*
*SUGGESTED READING*
*MATTHEW 6:33*

**³³ But seek first his kingdom and his righteousness, and all these things will be given to you as well. (NIV)**

Jesus tells us that we should first seek his kingdom and righteousness. This is the most important and best use of our time. With this being our priority, we will gain the wisdom of the Bible and better understand the will of God.

Once we accept this as what is important, all other things can be added as we feel they fit into our work for the Lord. We must be able to recognize what is made from this world can be distracting from our mission to spread the gospel.

DAY 3
SUGGESTED READING
JOHN 9:4

> **⁴ As long as it is day, we must do the works of him who sent me. Night is coming, when no one can work. (NIV)**

This is a metaphor on life and death. Day equates to the days of our life, as night equates to our death.

We must do what we can, with the time the Lord has given us, to do his work. Once we accept Christ, we should adopt his mission on earth to deliver the message of God to the non-believer.

What we do know is there is one physical life on Earth. Then, "And as it is appointed unto men once to die, but after this the judgment" (Hebrews 9:27 KJV). Do not waste time while we are alive. We only have a limited amount of time and we don't know how much there is of that.

DAY 4
SUGGESTED READING
MATTHEW 24:36

**³⁶ "But about that day or hour no one knows, not even the angels in heaven, nor the Son, but only the Father. (NIV)**

Christians know that the Lord will return. God has assigned a certain amount of time for man to seek redemption before he allows Christ to come and collect his children.

We have been told to be prepared for his return. Use our time to seek the wisdom of God. Don't get distracted in the ways of the world. Temptation comes in every form and some even appear worthwhile. But keep focused and pray on ambiguous situations.

DAY 5
SUGGESTED READING
JAMES 4:14

**¹⁴ Whereas ye know not what shall be on the morrow. For what is your life? It is even a vapour, that appeareth for a little time, and then vanisheth away. (KJV)**

It is presumptuous to talk of our future, but we do it all the time. Everything in our life is planned, for the most part, without consulting God. We should not be so arrogant.

In that we can be dead tomorrow, we must be prepared. We must use our time to understand the Will of God. We must be confident that we have done our best to be faithful and have followed the Law of the Lord. The message of this verse is recounted in Ben Sira Apocrypha; "As of the green leaves of a thick tree, some fall and some grow; so is the generation of flesh and blood: one cometh to an end and another is born" (Ben Sira 14:18 KJVA).

*DAY 6*
*SUGGESTED READING*
*COLOSSIANS 4:5*

**⁵ Be wise in the way you act toward outsiders; make the most of every opportunity. (NIV)**

Always be aware of the way we present to non-believers. They are listening and watching everything we say and do. If we are going to speak of God, we must be consistent in our talk. To have to change the story or to further explain the story is a waste of our time as the non-believer will see us as inconsistent and will have to be brought back around to our viewpoint.

Stay prepared. Read constantly to better understand the Word of God. Be consistent in your conversations with non-believers. This is the best way to make use of our time.

DAY 7
SUGGESTED READING
PROVERBS 21:5

**⁵ The plans of the diligent lead to profit as surely as haste leads to poverty. (NIV)**

There are no short cuts to understanding God's message. The more time spent reading the Bible and studying its content leads to rewards in spirit and posterity. Keep focused on the work that Jesus pursued while on Earth and try to do the same. Always keep your mind set on doing better work for God.

The opposite leads to temporary rewards at best. More likely than not, without God to assist in one's goals, failure reigns. Worse than that, there is no pathway to salvation without God's grace through Jesus. The unbeliever wastes his time on any pursuit that does not include working with God.

# WEEK 40
# OVERCOMING PREJUDICE

*Oscar C. Johnson PhD*

*DAY 1*
*SUGGESTED READING*
*GALATIANS 3:28*

**[28] There is neither Jew nor Gentile, neither slave nor free, nor is there male and female, for you are all one in Christ Jesus. (NIV)**

There is no favoritism in the eyes of the Lord once one is saved. Social rank, economic class or position does not make one better than another.

Deeper still is the fact that race nor gender separate those that are believers in Christ. We all receive the same gifts from God once we are saved. So be humble and be respecting of each other for we are all children of God.

What does matter, is whether you are saved or not. If one is not saved he is not recognized by God.

*DAY 2*
*SUGGESTED READING*
*JAMES 2:1 - 4*

**¹My brothers and sisters, believers in our glorious Lord Jesus Christ must not show favoritism.**

**² Suppose a man comes into your meeting wearing a gold ring and fine clothes, and a poor man in filthy old clothes also comes in.**

**³ If you show special attention to the man wearing fine clothes and say, "Here's a good seat for you," but say to the poor man, "You stand there" or "Sit on the floor by my feet,"**

**⁴ have you not discriminated among yourselves and become judges with evil thoughts? (NIV)**

In these verses James speaks out against favoritism. He explains that prejudice is just that, pre-judging someone without knowing their character. In these verses, he presents contrast between the rich and the poor.

It is very easy to favor those who look affluent as the world respects those that have accumulated riches. In almost every situation, the rich are always favored for no other reason than their looks. Who are we to judge? We must guard against this sin.

DAY 3
SUGGESTED READING
LEVITICUS 19:15

**¹⁵ "'Do not pervert justice; do not show partiality to the poor or favoritism to the great, but judge your neighbor fairly. (NIV)**

In the Old Testament God spoke to Moses about prejudice. He makes it clear that every person should be judged by Gods values not those of the world. The world makes heroes of the wealthy, the powerful, the athlete, the warrior. We should value people for different reasons than the world does.

Paul cautions the Christians in Corinth against regarding people from a worldly viewpoint. Look to the inside of people, especially the lowly and humble, for the presence of God. God is found in both the rich and powerful and the poor.

DAY 4
SUGGESTED READING
JAMES 2:9

**⁹ But if you show favoritism, you sin and are convicted by the law as lawbreakers. (NIV)**

Prejudice and Favoritism are both of the same cloth. Favoritism typically occurs when someone judges someone on appearance before getting to know them. It is difficult to overcome the adage, "You have one opportunity to make a first impression". Unfortunately, we all tend to use this as the barometer for judging people.

But Prejudice and Favoritism are sins. We may believe that we are not being prejudice and showing favoritism, so our sin may be overlooked. Sin in any form will keep one out of heaven. Pray for the ability to look at the man inwardly before making a judgement. This is how you would want to be judged.

DAY 5
SUGGESTED READING
1 SAMUEL 16:7

**⁷ But the LORD said to Samuel, "Do not consider his appearance or his height, for I have rejected him. The LORD does not look at the things people look at. People look at the outward appearance, but the LORD looks at the heart." (NIV)**

Samuel saw Eliab and assumed that he was chosen by God. He then saw seven other sons of Jesse and assumed that one of these has to be chosen by God. He was wrong on all counts.

When Jesse's last son, who was not even brought before him, was brought forth, God approved him. This son David, was a humble shepherd who was God fearing.

Samuel committed the sin of prejudice. He did not consider what was on the inside of the sons on Jesse. Samuel was looking at their outward appearances. God doesn't focus on appearances. He looks directly at the heart.

DAY 6
SUGGESTED READING
ROMANS 2:11

## **¹¹ For God does not show favoritism. (NIV)**

If one is saved through Jesus Christ, one is the same in God's eyes. The same gifts are afforded every Christian regardless of what works they do. The gifts of God are given by grace and cannot be taken away. So the rich an the poor are equal.

If there is any partiality that can be said about God, it is that he does not show favor to non-believers. This though, is not exactly God's choice but the choice of the non-believer. God offers his grace through salvation. The non-believer choses to rejects it.

DAY 7
SUGGESTED READING
ACTS 10:28

**²⁸ He said to them: "You are well aware that it is against our law for a Jew to associate with or visit a Gentile. But God has shown me that I should not call anyone impure or unclean. (NIV)**

The Jewish Pharisees were conflicted in Jesus's message that clearly broke tradition. The Jewish were the chosen people of God and did not associate with non-Jews. They had no reason other than tradition.

Jesus brought a new message. He did not show prejudice to any man in any form. He also commanded that we love one another as we love ourselves. The only higher commandment is to love God.

# WEEK 41
# PRIDE

*DAY 1*
*SUGGESTED READING*
*ISAIAH 2:12*

**¹² The LORD Almighty has a day in store**
**for all the proud and lofty,**
**for all that is exalted**
**(and they will be humbled), (NIV)**

It has been said that pride may be the source of all sin. We are all proud of our accomplishments. We tend to brag about this to others. This is where we get in trouble. Be proud to yourself. The Lord knows what you have accomplished, and he is proud of you. Take stock in yourself and be humble in your accomplishments. Give praise to the Lord for them.

God despises pride. What is prideful to man brings punishment from God. The Bible references how He will bring down the prideful in multiple places. All things that create a prideful nature will be humbled on the day of judgement.

*DAY 2*
*SUGGESTED READING*
*JAMES 4:6*

**⁶ But he gives us more grace. That is why Scripture says:**

**"God opposes the proud
but shows favor to the humble." (NIV)**

God always has grace to give. This is especially true for the unbeliever. That grace is starts with the gift of salvation. For the believer, God has more grace to give. His grace is infinite and inexhaustible.

Be proud but be humble. God knows what you are doing. You can never exhaust his grace. Interesting enough is the fact that God will give more grace when we rely on him more. When we are at our weakest. (Read 2 Corinthians 12:9)

On the other hand, the more we rely on our own ways and thinking, the less God will avail us with his grace. Pride will not help us in the day of judgement.

*DAY 3*
*SUGGESTED READING*
*JEREMIAH 9:23*

**²³ This is what the LORD says:**

**"Let not the wise boast of their wisdom
or the strong boast of their strength
or the rich boast of their riches, (NIV)**

God makes it very clear what he feels about pride. He tells us specifically not to be prideful. All the things that man acknowledges as being great is great only to man. God does not care about mans riches, power, popularity or successes.

Not to say that there aren't believers who have achieved all these things. They to are available by God for his glorification. Christians thus blessed must be wary of letting pride take hold. Remember all these things are given by God and praise should be given to him.

*DAY 4*
*SUGGESTED READING*
*PROVERBS 11:2*

**² When pride comes, then comes disgrace,
but with humility comes wisdom. (NIV)**

The proud person is one who thinks he is better than others. He thinks everyone views him as he views himself. What he can't seem to understand is that people typically despise those who are self-indulged. More importantly, God also does not care for the proud.

Conversely, the humble does not need to advertise their accomplishments granted by God. They are strong in faith and modest. The humble gives praise to God and knows God's will through constant study of his Word. This person is liked by man and favored by God.

*DAY 5*
*SUGGESTED READING*
*PSALM 10:4*

**⁴ In his pride the wicked man does not seek him;
in all his thoughts there is no room for God. (NIV)**

The proud is proud because they are consumed by making themselves favorable to the world. They want all to see their accomplishments. In doing this, they have no time to dwell on the Lord.

The proud does not feel that God is responsible for their success. They have worked hard for what they have attained and deserve credit for it. The proud are not seeking God because they are consumed with what is important to man.

DAY 6
SUGGESTED READING
ROMANS 12:3

> **³ For by the grace given me I say to every one of you: Do not think of yourself more highly than you ought, but rather think of yourself with sober judgment, in accordance with the faith God has distributed to each of you. (NIV)**

Paul tells the Christians of Rome to not engage in pride. It is easy to think that one has more status with God because they are Christian and are better than others as a result.

We are always in danger of showing our pride as Christians and disparage others who are not. This is a sin. God does not show partiality.

More to fellow Christians than non-believers is this concept more appropriate. We should not think we are favored more in Gods eyes because of the way we are used. We all are given gifts according to how God will use us. Let others speak of our character. Let them recognize the gifts God has bestowed on you and be happy for you.

DAY 7
SUGGESTED READING
OBADIAH 1:3 - 4

> ³ **The pride of your heart has deceived you,
> you who live in the clefts of the rocks
> and make your home on the heights,
> you who say to yourself,
> 'Who can bring me down to the ground?'**
>
> ⁴ **Though you soar like the eagle
> and make your nest among the stars,
> from there I will bring you down,"
> declares the LORD. (NIV)**

There are those who think that they are so powerful that they cannot be assailed by anyone or anything. Everything that they have gained is gained in the ways of man. They did not acknowledge God in their efforts and have no room for him now that they have risen above other men. Their hearts are hardened to God. They have lost all humility.

God is the answer to this folly. People like this have earned the displeasure of God and are punished as a result of their pride. Those who over-estimate themselves can look forward to eventual destruction and in the eyes of God will have no intrinsic value because they have no faith in what is most important; God's glory.

# WEEK 42
# GOD'S HELP

DAY 1
SUGGESTED READING
ISAIAH 41:10

**¹⁰ So do not fear, for I am with you;
do not be dismayed, for I am your God.
I will strengthen you and help you;
I will uphold you with my righteous right hand.
(NIV)**

God gives us encouragement in this verse. He wants us to know that he is with us and therefore do not fear. There ae times when we feel that we cannot move forward because we are being assailed by things we cannot control. The world does not care about justice or righteousness. It will devour us if we try to take it on alone.

Through prayer, God will protect us. He is our refuge and shelter. He is sovereign over all that is in the Universe and cares for the smallest insect to his greatest creation, us. He wants us to bring our problems to him and he will do what is best for us.

*DAY 2*
*SUGGESTED READING*
*PROVERBS 3:5-6*

> **⁵ Trust in the LORD with all your heart**
> **and lean not on your own understanding;**
> **⁶ in all your ways submit to him,**
> **and he will make your paths straight (NIV)**

When trouble strikes, we want to make the right decisions. We want to feel like we are in control of our lives and can navigate through the worldly evils that surround. Nonetheless, some things are beyond our ability to solve.

This is where we must trust in the Lord. He sees the whole picture and knows what is best for us. To trust with all our heart means to not rely on whatever we think is best for us but to accept whatever God decides for us. God will guide us.

God sees things different than we do. His thoughts are not of this world and not affected by this world. Where worldly solutions can be right or wrong, God's decisions never change and are always right. It must be, or He would be imperfect.

Everyone has the ability to chose how to live their life. Relying on ourselves is risking failure and bad decisions. God wants us to rely on him and he will help us.

DAY 3
SUGGESTED READING
HEBREW 13:6

**⁶ So we say with confidence,**

**"The Lord is my helper; I will not be afraid.
What can mere mortals do to me?" (NIV)**

God promised to always be there for his people long ago, "Never will I leave you; never will I forsake you." (Hebrews 13:5 NIV) This commitment stands today as then. God will provide for us for whatever we need.

Being Christian, we are spiritually equipped to deal with life's trials. The Holy Spirit is given to us to help us endure all the world assaults on us. Pray for God's help and rest assured that He will answer. It may not be as fast as we want but it will come. God knows what is best for us and will not let us fail or be overwhelmed by the trials of the world.

*DAY 4*
*SUGGESTED READING*
*1CORINTHIANS 10:13*

**¹³ No temptation has overtaken you except what is common to mankind. And God is faithful; he will not let you be tempted beyond what you can bear. But when you are tempted, he will also provide a way out so that you can endure it. (NIV)**

Everyone is subject to temptations. This includes believers and non-believers alike. The temptations are all pathways to sin. Since no one is exempt from the lure of sin, nothing is unique.

When temptation occurs, there are worldly solutions to satisfy the urge. These can be acceptable by worldly standards but unacceptable by the morals of God.

God is aware of the temptations of man. He promises to not make the temptation more than what we can handle. He will always provide a way to endure our temptations. Pray when being tempted. Pray for strength and walk away if you can. God will reward you for your faith.

*DAY 5*
*SUGGESTED READING*
*JOHN 15:7*

> **⁷ If ye abide in me, and my words abide in you, ye shall ask what ye will, and it shall be done unto you. (KJV)**

Yes, God will answer our prayers, but it is conditional. Jesus will bring our prayers to God but only if they are in accordance with the nature of God. We cannot ask for things that are used for pleasure or to take advantage of another. God wants to help us, but He will not listen to frivolous request.

God will also not listen to us if we are harboring sin in our hearts. He knows that we are not perfect, but he expects us to live as piously as we can and control our conduct and emotions. Prayer is not telling God what to do, but is should be presented with an attitude of dependency and need. Always keep in mind what God is and know that he will do what is best for us, not what we think is good for us.

*DAY 6*
*SUGGESTED READING*
*1 PETER 5:7*

# **⁷ Cast all your anxiety on him because he cares for you. (NIV)**

There are times when we are troubled. These can encompass family, employment, the future, sins of our past, legal, loss, illness, the list is unending. When we are struggling with any of these events we can easily become anxious or depressed. We may pray for God's help as we try to find our way out of the disarray that is torturing us.

God tells us what to do in these situations. Not only in Peter but in Psalms and Isaiah he tells us to bring our problems to him. Our lack of faith is what causes our anxiety. Our lack of faith implies some distrust that God will deliver us from our situation.

God cares for us. He wants us to depend on Him when things are troubling an we have no answers. To not trust him is a sin because we are trying to find something else that we can trust to deliver us. He tells us he cares for us and no matter what the situation is, He will take the burden. This was part of Christ purpose, to relieve us of worldly troubles and give us God's peace.

Give all our troubles to God. Be strong in faith because he will do what is best for us. If we do this, we will be relieved of our anxiety knowing that God will give us his grace and strength.

DAY 7
SUGGESTED READING
JEREMIAH 32:27

> ²⁷ **Behold, I am the LORD, the God of all flesh: is there anything too hard for me? (KJV)**

This question that God posed to Jeremiah is simple and rhetorical. Of course, it seems that there is nothing that God can't do. He can help in any situation and solve any problem because he is sovereign over the Universe. God is there to provide for us. He created us and favored us over the angels. He is happy when we acknowledge him in all our doings. He listens and answers our prayers when we believe and have faith in him.

But there are some things that God can't do. God cannot lie. He cannot be wrong. He cannot be aware of any situation. He can't change. If he did any of these things he would not be omnipotent. This would destroy the whole purpose of the Bible and giving our lives, heart, mind and soul to him. Praise be to the Lord for being unable to do these things.

# WEEK 43
# SEEKING STRENGTH

DAY 1
SUGGESTED READING
JEREMIAH 29:13

> **¹³ You will seek me and find me when you seek me with all your heart. (NIV)**

When we seek God in Christ, he will hear our prayers. To often we do not use this resource as we try to find answers on our own. As a Christian, we are told to rely on God and bring him our problems. If we seek his help with belief and faith, he will come to our aid.

To the non-believer, the message of this verse can be life changing. Those who are seeking God through Jesus will find him and be saved. They will get the advantage of the Holy Spirit an enjoy the gifts of God.

*DAY 2*
*SUGGESTED READING*
*ISAIAH 41:10*

**[10] So do not fear, for I am with you;**
**do not be dismayed, for I am your God.**
**I will strengthen you and help you;**
**I will uphold you with my righteous right hand.**
**(NIV)**

The Lord gives us encourage with this verse. It is challenging to live the Christian life. The world is constantly tempting us with sin. Our adversaries are constantly willing to argue with us about our belief.

Stay strong. Praise the Lord for delivering us from the evils of the world. Our faith will strengthen us.

*DAY 3*
*SUGGESTED READING*
*PHILIPPIANS 4:13*

**¹³ I can do all this through him who gives me strength. (NIV)**

Paul makes this statement, but it is not to be taken literally. The message to the Christian is that things can be accomplished if it is God's will. There is nothing wrong with self-sufficiency, just remember to acknowledge God who gives you strength.

If it is God's Will, we surely can accomplish anything.

*DAY 4*
*SUGGESTED READING*
*2 THESSALONIANS 3:3*

**³ But the Lord is faithful, and he will strengthen you and protect you from the evil one. (NIV)**

The Lord is faithful. This is a promise that we as Christians can rely on. Man cannot be trusted because he is fallible, but we know that God is not.

Satan will tempt us and attack us in many different forms. He wants to weaken our faith and belief in the Lord. He attacks us more than he does non-believers. They are already his servants. He satisfies their needs with instant gratification and temporary rewards to keep them loyal.

As we recognize these attacks, we realize that God is there through the Holy Spirit giving us the resolve to make the right decisions. The more we trust God, the more we are aware of His faithfulness is towards us. Without Him we would be consumed by evil.

DAY 5
SUGGESTED READING
1 CORINTHIANS 1:18

**[18] For the message of the cross is foolishness to those who are perishing, but to us who are being saved it is the power of God. (NIV)**

Being saved opens the door to the graces of God. There is unlimited power in these graces and this power strengthens as our faith strengthens.

We must not be selfish in our faith. We should have love and compassion for those who do not feel the Holy Spirit within them. It is part of our duty to share the gospel of Jesus to the unsaved.

DAY 6
SUGGESTED READING
1 CHRONICLES 16:11

**¹¹ Look to the LORD and his strength;
seek his face always. (NIV)**

Never forget what God has done. He has created the Universe. Greater still, He has created life. God gives us the standard for righteous living and shows us his devotion to us through the sacrifice of his son for our sins.

God will never turn his back on us. He wants to help us in all our situations. He promises strength. Acknowledge God in all that you do. Trust in Him always. There is no other source in the Universe that can do what he can.

DAY 7
SUGGESTED READING
PSALM 29:11

## [11] The LORD gives strength to his people; the LORD blesses his people with peace. (NIV)

The Lord makes the Christian life bearable in a world that is dominated by Sin. Through prayer, we can ask the Lord for strength and perseverance in any situation. Our faith ensures the blessings of the Lord and we rely on them to deliver us.

Trust in the Lord. It will make your life much easier to navigate. When you leave decisions to God, you can rest assured that you will make the right choices. Through prayer, the Holy Spirit will guide you.

# WEEK 44
# ANGER

*DAY 1*
*SUGGESTED READING*
*PROVERBS 29:11*

**[11] Fools give full vent to their rage,
but the wise bring calm in the end. (NIV)**

Anger is one of our strongest emotions. It is not a sin to be angry, but it can lead to sinful thoughts and behaviors. It also leads to loss of control. This leads to revealing all that is in one's mind. The danger is that venting like this may cause harms that cannot be repaired.

Keep your emotions under control. Think about the source of your anger and discuss it rationally in the right time.

DAY 2
SUGGESTED READING
PROVERBS 15:1

**15 A gentle answer turns away wrath,
but a harsh word stirs up anger. (NIV)**

Anger will typically start arguments. Arguments will frequently spin out of control and cause all involved to further escalate the anger. Irrational thinking and speech is the end result in these situations. Satan relishes these situations. This is and perfect opportunity for sin to take control.

Cooler heads realize that uncontrolled anger will not solve problems. Gentleness is the best way to disarm the most contentious arguments. Always keep in mind that one angry word produces another.

DAY 3
SUGGESTED READING
PROVERBS 22:24

**²⁴ Do not make friends with a hot-tempered person,
do not associate with one easily angered, (NIV)**

The person who cannot control his affections is a dangerous person to be around. This person will say things that are sinful and evil. They will also say things to you that are hurtful and may incite anger in you.

Do not make friends with this person but always treat them with gentleness. Let them see your spirit through your behavior and speech.

DAY 4
SUGGESTED READING
JAMES 1:20

**²⁰ for the anger of man does not produce the righteousness of God. (ESV)**

Anger and righteousness are in contrast with each other. Anger can lead to sin where righteousness is in line with the Will of God. Christians cannot be righteous if they are harboring anger in their heart.

It is not a sin to be angry. Who cannot be angry when injustice occurs? When exploitation happens to those who cannot defend themselves? In these circumstances it is right to be angry. Ephesians tells us, "Be angry, and do not sin" (Ephesians 4:26 KJV). Anger will give Satan an opportunity to enter our lives. Anger can be strong or weak. Understand your anger, pray for a way to soften it, and forgive the transgressor. The Lord will judge in His own time.

DAY 5
SUGGESTED READING
GENESIS 4:5 - 8

> **⁵ but for Cain and his offering he had no regard. So Cain was very angry, and his face fell.**
>
> **⁶ The L&#xff;ORD said to Cain, "Why are you angry, and why has your face fallen?**
>
> **⁷ If you do well, will you not be accepted? And if you do not do well, sin is crouching at the door. Its desire is contrary to you, but you must rule over it."**
>
> **⁸ Cain spoke to Abel his brother. And when they were in the field, Cain rose up against his brother Abel and killed him. (ESV)**

This is the classic case of inappropriate anger. Cain was angry because his offering to God was not accepted. God told him that some underlying sin was the reason for the unacceptance. God even told him that he needs to correct and control the sin. Instead of listening to God, Cain's anger led him to kill his brother as if this would solve his problem.

If we do not control our anger, we are in danger of making horrible decisions. These poor decisions can lead to life altering consequences. Festering anger clouds good judgement and makes it hard to maintain righteousness. When we have unresolved anger for whatever reason, pray for understanding and a change of heart. The Bible has the answer as to what is righteous and unrighteous anger. Faith will get your through these difficult times.

DAY 6
SUGGESTED READING
PROVERBS 14:29

**²⁹ He that is slow to wrath is of great understanding: but he that is hasty of spirit exalteth folly. (KJV)**

Anger is an unhealthy emotion and has caused the worse events to happen in the world. It does the same in our lives. It is a response to a stimulus that is typically self-centered. Our egos want us to be in control and if we don't have that control we want to punish those who won't give it to us. As a result, bad decisions are made hastily or deviously planned. Either way, the decision will be resented in the end.

Regardless of the anger, Christians should contemplate the reason for it. First, one should not respond to an anger situation with snap decisions. Second, know that anger will most likely result in sin. Third, consult the Bible and pray for understanding. Ask for help from the Lord in finding resolution that is most expedient and causes the least harm.

DAY 7
SUGGESTED READING
EPHESIANS 4:26 - 27

**²⁶ "In your anger do not sin": Do not let the sun go down while you are still angry,**

**²⁷ and do not give the devil a foothold. (NIV)**

All anger is not sin. Anger can serve a purpose and ultimately cause good. Though the temptation is to give in to bitterness, stay focused and resist. Giving in is the pathway to sin.

Christians believe that God is in control of their life. Not trusting in God is the worse thing that they could do. When we try to resolve anger issues ourselves, we are not believing in God's control and love for us. Even when anger is just, we mustn't hold on to it to long. The longer we do, the risk of sin increases. Just anger unresolved can lead to resentment.

The situation that has caused the anger has happened. It cannot be recalled. The best we can do is to manage the anger. Evaluate the situation from all angles and try to deal with it without anger. This act in itself will start to defuse the situation. This is the righteous way and is in accordance with God's Will.

# WEEK 45
# DISCOURAGED

*DAY 1*
*SUGGESTED READING*
*JOSHUA 1:9*

> **⁹ Have I not commanded you? Be strong and courageous. Do not be afraid; do not be discouraged, for the LORD your God will be with you wherever you go." (NIV)**

There are many times that we feel discouraged and don't know how to proceed in life. Life is difficult, and nothing is given to us. In our attempts to weather the difficulties we become overwhelmed and afraid.

God commands us to not despair. He tells us to rely on him for strength and guidance. He promises to always be with us no matter how challenging times are. This promise is something that we can rely on because His Word is truth. We, as Christians, should be encouraged in these promises. We should trust in God always without question.

*Day 2*
SUGGESTED READING
Luke 18:1

## 18 Then Jesus told his disciples a parable to show them that they should always pray and not give up. (NIV)

God has told us on multiple occasions that we should not be discouraged and pray for his strength and courage. The parable that Jesus tells his disciples is one of these occasions.

A judge that is a non-believer was confronted by a widow asking for justice against an adversary. Initially, he ignored her and would not entertain her plea. She continued to return to him repeatedly pleading her case. He eventually, had enough and granted her justice.

The point of this parable is that if an unbeliever can be enticed to listen and grant justice, how much more would God listen to his children who ask for his help. God wants us to bring our problems to him in pray and he will answer them in his time and according to his will.

DAY 3
SUGGESTED READING
PHILIPPIANS 4:4 - 6

**⁴ Rejoice in the Lord always. I will say it again: Rejoice!**

**⁵ Let your gentleness be evident to all. The Lord is near.**

**⁶ Do not be anxious about anything, but in every situation, by prayer and petition, with thanksgiving, present your requests to God. (NIV)**

Paul gives us words of encouragement. We need to trust in the Lord in all that we do and acknowledge him in all that we do. God has promised to be our strength and our refuge. We just need to present our prayers to him with belief that he will answer them.

Give thanks to God that we have someone who is there for us in all situations. Praise him for his grace an unwavering faithfulness to us.

*DAY 4*
*SUGGESTED READING*
*ROMANS 8:28*

**²⁸ And we know that in all things God works for the good of those who love him, who have been called according to his purpose. (NIV)**

Christians are called by God. Not only have heard the Word but responded with their belief and faith. The reasoning is that God has a purpose for them.

None knows the exact purpose of God but what Christians do know is that God's plan is only good for those who are his chosen. Of His plan, Christians do know that they are to deliver the gospel of Christ. They must share their faith to the non-believers. They must also conduct their life in a way that represents righteousness.

Though we share our faith, it goes without saying that the majority of people will not listen. This is hard for us to take as we know the consequences of their decisions. This, at times, is discouraging. But we should not despair and pray for strength to continue. God is there with us always.

DAY 5
SUGGESTED READING
JEREMIAH 29:11

**[11] For I know the plans I have for you," declares the Lord, "plans to prosper you and not to harm you, plans to give you hope and a future. (NIV)**

Our faith will not go unrewarded. This is a promise of God. Though life can be challenging and discouraging He has a plan for us and it does not include a life of want and pain.

We must keep the faith and do God's work. We all have different gifts from God and must use them accordingly. Do not envy another's gift because it is for us to have our own and them to have theirs. We all fit into God's plan.

*DAY 6*
*SUGGESTED READING*
*GALATIANS 6:9*

**⁹ Let us not become weary in doing good, for at the proper time we will reap a harvest if we do not give up. (NIV)**

In life, we are confronted with continuing pressures on a daily basis. Additionally, we have the pressure of living a pious life and presenting this image to man always. We can only take so much before we start to weary and start to not care.

God knows that these pressures build but wants us to remain persistent in doing good. We too must be aware that the pressure is building and pray for strength to continue. God will not let our problems get so great that we cannot overcome them. We just need to keep God involved and He will see us through.

*Day 7*
SUGGESTED READING
PHILIPPIANS 3:13 - 14

**[13] Brothers and sisters, I do not consider myself yet to have taken hold of it. But one thing I do: Forgetting what is behind and straining toward what is ahead,**

**[14] I press on toward the goal to win the prize for which God has called me heavenward in Christ Jesus. (NIV)**

Something may have happened in your life that significantly is holding you back. That is making it difficult to think about God and God's plan for you. If this has happened to you or is happening to you, it must be confronted, or it can consume you.

God wants us to move forward. We must grow to move forward. This requires us to forget our past. Spiritual growth is a constant process of moving forward. Study God's Word always that you can continue to grow.

# WEEK 46
# BELIEF

*DAY 1*
*SUGGESTE READING*
*JOHN 20:29*

**²⁹ Then Jesus told him, "Because you have seen me, you have believed; blessed are those who have not seen and yet have believed." (NIV)**

People are doubting by nature. We are constantly told many things that are supposed to be true that end up false. As a result, we want evidence. Not only to be told about something, but to actually see the evidence. If not in person, then we want to be told by someone that is generally trusted to be credible.

In the time of Christ, we had Him is person and his apostles. One could seek Christ message by going to the sources. Today we have the Bible. We can go to the Bible at any time to seek the message of Christ. We can seek the message of Christ in church.

Just as we can accept that there is gravity or electricity by being told by experts that the evidence of their existence is in the science, we can believe that Jesus's message is true from the experts that are Christians. We see neither, but we believe that they are true.

DAY 2
SUGGESTED READING
ROMANS 10:9 - 10

**⁹ If you declare with your mouth, "Jesus is Lord," and believe in your heart that God raised him from the dead, you will be saved.**

**¹⁰ For it is with your heart that you believe and are justified, and it is with your mouth that you profess your faith and are saved. (NIV)**

To the unbeliever, Jesus is not who Christians claim him to be. This may not be only agnostics and atheist, but also from other religions. They all do not believe he is the son of God and the Messiah.

The unbeliever must come to God through Jesus and this starts with belief. Christians must be patient with the unbeliever when delivering the gospel of Jesus. The importance of belief must be explained in a way that the unbelievers heart and soul are touched by the Holy Spirit.

Help the unbeliever come to the realization that God has a purpose for their life and believing in Jesus is the way to giving them understanding that life has meaning and the path to salvation.

*DAY 3*
*SUGGESTED READING*
*MARK 16:15 - 16*

**¹⁵ He said to them, "Go into all the world and preach the gospel to all creation.**

**¹⁶ Whoever believes and is baptized will be saved, but whoever does not believe will be condemned. (NIV)**

This was the last command of Jesus before he left Earth to preside at the right hand of his father in Heaven. His doctrine on Earth was over for that time. He had taught his disciples what they needed to know to deliver the message of God.

The message is powerful in that the command admonishes all Christians to spread the gospel. The message to unbelievers is to believe that they may be saved. Without belief they will be condemned. We don't have Jesus with us physically, but we have the Bible as evidence of God's truth.

DAY 4
SUGGESTED READING
1 JOHN 4:1 - 2

**¹Dear friends, do not believe every spirit, but test the spirits to see whether they are from God, because many false prophets have gone out into the world.**

**² This is how you can recognize the Spirit of God: Every spirit that acknowledges that Jesus Christ has come in the flesh is from God, (NIV)**

There are many beliefs being preached in the world today. These beliefs have followers in small and large numbers. There is belief if God but see no need for Jesus. Some believe that Jesus existed but was not from God. Others worship various idols that have no connection to God. Then there are science-based religions. People are trying to make sense out of this world and will listen to whatever makes the most sense to them.

We must guard against false teachings and put all the teachings to the Biblical test. There is only one true God and one true Jesus and Jesus comes in the flesh from God. Anything that does not acknowledge this fundamental truth is false.

DAY 5
SUGGESTED READING
LEVITICUS 19:31

**³¹ "'Do not turn to mediums or seek out spiritists, for you will be defiled by them. I am the LORD your God. (NIV)**

Believers and non-believers should take heed to verse. From the early times of polytheism, there has been those who entered pacts with Satan and have been granted power to entice people to the ways of evil and sin.

Anyone that succumbs to this evil will surely be condemned. Through them, there is no path to salvation. Through them, will ultimately lead to ruin while on Earth and rejection by God.

DAY 6
SUGGESTED READING
HEBREWS 11:6

**⁶And without faith it is impossible to please God, because anyone who comes to him must believe that he exists and that he rewards those who earnestly seek him. (NIV)**

First and foremost, we must believe in God. Without belief nothing else can proceed. Once we believe then we can live of lives through faith. For those who believe, God will always be with them. This he promises.

If we doubt the existence of God in the slightest, we need to re-evaluate what we do believe in. Without belief our faith is meaningless. It is true that we cannot see him, but we must believe that he is. Our belief is strengthened with prayer and study of his Word. The more we believe, the stronger our faith and the more faith we have in him, the more faith he will have in us.

DAY 7
SUGGESTED READING
JAMES 1:6

**⁶ But when you ask, you must believe and not doubt, because the one who doubts is like a wave of the sea, blown and tossed by the wind. (NIV)**

"If you believe, you will receive whatever you ask for in prayer." (Matthew 21:22 NIV) God wants to answer our prayers. We must have no doubt in this, for doubt is disbelief.

What this requires is steadfast faith. As a Christian, faith is what our belief is based on. Faith connects us with the power of God. We have faith that God has certain traits that include truth, perfection, wisdom and righteousness. If God says that he will answer our prayers, then we must accept this as fact.

# WEEK 47
# FEAR

*DAY 1*
*SUGGESTED READING*
*ISAIAH 41:10*

**¹⁰ So do not fear, for I am with you;**
**do not be dismayed, for I am your God.**
**I will strengthen you and help you;**
**I will uphold you with my righteous right hand.**
**(NIV)**

God is our protector. He consoles us with this promise that he will be there to be our refuge.

We must keep this in mind as we struggle with fear. It is reality that we will fear, but we must not let it consume us. Satan wants us to be overwhelmed by fear. This is a foothold for him to entice us to solutions that sway away from righteousness. Overwhelming fear will create dark places in our mind which can control our behavior.

God wants us to have faith in his power over fear. He promises to assist us in our struggles with fear. He is sovereign over Earth and the Heavens. None is stronger than he.

*DAY 2*
*SUGGESTED READING*
*PHILIPPIANS 4:6 - 7*

**⁶ Do not be anxious about anything, but in every situation, by prayer and petition, with thanksgiving, present your requests to God.**

**⁷ And the peace of God, which transcends all understanding, will guard your hearts and your minds in Christ Jesus. (NIV)**

Fear and anxiety go hand in hand. We experience both in all aspects of our life. They can be of minimal significance or overwhelming to the point of paralyzing us. Modern medicine provides solutions with medication to help manage our fear and anxiety. These may help temporarily. However, chemical solutions are not cures for emotional problems.

God tells us to bring our problems to Him through his son and our advocate, Jesus. Pray with faith that the Lord will answer our prayers. Give thanks that He is there to answer our prayers. This is a promise of God. It cannot be broken or refused. We may not know how it will come about but that is the power of God. He knows all and can affect any situation according to his will.

*DAY 3*
*SUGGESTED READING*
*1 JOHN 4:18*

**¹⁸ There is no fear in love. But perfect love drives out fear, because fear has to do with punishment. The one who fears is not made perfect in love. (NIV)**

According to Wikipedia, "Fear in human beings may occur in response to a specific stimulus occurring in the present, or in anticipation or expectation of a future threat perceived as a risk to body or life." Very little can be done to avoid this condition. Everybody handles fear differently.

John tells us that there is no need to fear. He tells us of God's infinite love for us that drives out fear. God is all powerful and will not suffer his children to suffer from fear. If he loves us, he will not let us be overcome with fear. We must pray when we are afraid. We must ask him to be with us that we have confidence in overcoming what is making us afraid.

*DAY 4*
*SUGGESTED READING*
*ISAIAH 43:1*

**¹ But now, this is what the Lord says—**
**he who created you, Jacob,**
**he who formed you, Israel:**
**"Do not fear, for I have redeemed you;**
**I have summoned you by name; you are mine.**
**(NIV)**

God call Jacob and the people of Israel to him. He tells them not to fear. He does this today, to all who receive him.

Just as it was then, The Lord will be with us through all our troubles and predicaments. He reassures us of his power in that he created all that there is. What can stand against this power?

DAY 5
SUGGESTED READING
PSALM 27:1

> ¹ The LORD is my light and my salvation—
> whom shall I fear?
> The LORD is the stronghold of my life—
> of whom shall I be afraid? (NIV)

The Christian has nothing to fear. They have nothing to fear today or in the future. Even death is not something to fear as we have been promised salvation.

As we face the challenges of life, we can move forward in confidence knowing that the Lord is there to protect and guide us. This is a promise which cannot be broken.

*DAY 6*
*SUGGESTED READING*
*ISAIAH 41:13 - 14*

> **¹³ For I, the L**ORD **your God,**
> **will hold your right hand,**
> **saying to you, "Do not fear;**
> **I will help you."**
> **¹⁴ Do not fear, you worm Jacob,**
> **and you men of Israel.**
> **I will help you, says the L**ORD
> **and your Redeemer, the Holy One of Israel.**
> **(MEV)**

The Lord encourages us with these verses. He promises his help and tells us not to fear. As insignificant as we are, he will not abandon us.

The Lord knows what we need. He wants us to rely on him and trust him. If we do this, we will not be afraid.

DAY 7
SUGGESTED READING
PSALM 56:3 - 4

**³ When I am afraid, I put my trust in you.**

**⁴ In God, whose word I praise—
in God I trust and am not afraid.
What can mere mortals do to me? (NIV)**

The world of man is filled with awful things. At times these things affect our lives. In those times it is natural to become afraid. We fear because we do not know the outcome of the darkness that is enveloping our minds.

Satan uses our fear against. When we are focused on what can harm us we are not thinking about God. This is when we need to think about God the most. We pray, we trust and refuse to be afraid.

We may still be afraid, but we have faith that God is with us. We may not have control, but we know that God is. We may not know what will happen in the future, but we know that God has a plan and we are part of it.

# WEEK 48
# RELATIONSHIP WITH GOD

*DAY 1*
*SUGGESTED READING*
*RELEVATION 3:20*

**²⁰ Here I am! I stand at the door and knock. If anyone hears my voice and opens the door, I will come in and eat with that person, and they with me. (NIV)**

To the believer, we must work on our relationship with God. It is easy to get involved with work, family and other commitments and not spend time with God. This is dangerous as God is always there and we are refusing to let him in.

To the non-believer, the opportunity is being presented. It can be presented multiple times. The non-believer must take the initiative and open the door. If done, He will come in. He will forgive all their sins and impart the Holy Spirit upon them.

God loves us and will always be there if we let him in. We need to be receptive to his knocking. He knows our troubles and needs. Building a strong relationship with God gives us a companion to share our lives with.

DAY 2
SUGGESTED READING
JOHN 6:40

**⁴⁰ For my Father's will is that everyone who looks to the Son and believes in him shall have eternal life, and I will raise them up at the last day." (NIV)**

God's will is that we believe in Jesus and build a relationship with him. He is not asking us to do remarkable things to show the world that we one of his children, he just wants us to believe in Jesus and wants us to get to know him above all else. The reward is not in earthly position and power but in salvation on the last day. Jesus made this requirement simple so that all can benefit.

We are used to doing things in order to benefit. In this world this is how we succeed. It is difficult for us to believe that we will get something for nothing. But we should not try to figure out why and how God does this for us. We must believe and trust that it will happen as he promises.

DAY 3
SUGGESTED READING
JOHN 15:5

**⁵ "I am the vine; you are the branches. If you remain in me and I in you, you will bear much fruit; apart from me you can do nothing. (NIV)**

Jesus explains the importance of building a relationship with us and God through Him. He is the source of God's will. His message is directly from God. Building a relationship with Jesus makes us want to be more like him and act like him.

The result of this relationship is producing more believers. And as we know, God wants to save all that are willing to follow in the way of Jesus's righteousness. But without him we can do nothing. Without knowing and living with Jesus there is no way to bring people to God. Anything we say will not be taken seriously if our words are not matched with spiritual guidance. People know when someone is faking conviction. The saying is, "their heart is not in it".

DAY 4
SUGGESTED READING
ACTS 3:19

**¹⁹ Repent, then, and turn to God, so that your sins may be wiped out, that times of refreshing may come from the Lord, (NIV)**

God has always wanted a relationship with his creation, Man. He was saddened when Adam trusted Satan and not him in the garden of Eden. That all Man is burdened with Adam's sin, Man's relationship with him was severed. This was a choice Adam made condemning us all.

But God gives us another choice. He sent his Son to sacrifice himself for our sins. Accepting Christ and his message from God is the choice God provides us to re-establish our relationship with him. This is the message that all Christians must offer the unsaved.

DAY 5
SUGGESTED READING
ROMANS 6:23

**²³ For the wages of sin is death, but the gift of God is eternal life in Christ Jesus our Lord. (NIV)**

This is the signally the most important reason for a relationship with God. All have sinned. None can enter Heaven if they have sin.

God offers an uncomplicated way to rectify this situation. It is free. That means there are no strings attached. He wants us to believe in his son and accept him as Lord. Jesus cleanses us of all sin. This act alone will allow us salvation. Establishing this relationship changes us in a way that brings us closer to God. Through prayer and study of the Bible this relationship grows stronger.

*DAY 6*
*SUGGESTED READING*
*2 TIMOTHY 1:7*

**⁷ For the Spirit God gave us does not make us timid, but gives us power, love and self-discipline. (NIV)**

When we have a relationship with God we become changed. God improves our attitude and gives us confidence. We see things more clearly as we are not confused or consumed with earthly pursuits.

We understand that there will be trials set before us, but we also know that we have the Lord with us to get us through them. This requires continual communication with Him and involving Him in all that we do. God will do his share if we do ours. It is like any other relationship we develop.

DAY 7
SUGGESTED READING
PROVERBS 3:5 - 6

**⁵ Trust in the LORD with all thine heart; and lean not unto thine own understanding.**

**⁶ In all thy ways acknowledge him, and he shall direct thy paths. (KJV)**

God wants us to have a relationship of total trust. The Christian knows this from multiple sources in the Bible. Moses had no choice but to trust God as he led his people out of Egypt. But God trusted him also. Moses and God had a strong relationship. They were in constant contact with each other.

Moses trusted God with all the decisions that he made for his people. He did not understand what God's intention was in certain situations, but he did as he was instructed, and things would turn out good.

This is the message of these verses. We must trust in the Lord with all our heart. Let God direct our decision making and the events of our life. We will likely fail if we attempt to leave God out of the equation. Besides, not involving God is surely not having a relationship with the one being that has sovereignty over the universe. Not having a relationship with God who wants to have one with us is reckless. The LORD replied to Moses, "Whoever has sinned against me I will blot out of my book." (Exodus 32:33)

# WEEK 49
# RELATIONSHIPS WITH OTHERS

DAY 1
SUGGESTED READING
JOHN 13:34

> **[34] "A new command I give you: Love one another. As I have loved you, so you must love one another. (NIV)**

This command seems to be the same as what the Lord commanded in Leviticus, "Do not seek revenge or bear a grudge against anyone among your people but love your neighbor as yourself. I am the LORD." (Leviticus 19:18)

Closer inspection of this has a more profound impact. Jesus tells his disciples to love each other as He loved them. Jesus loved Man so much that he gave his life for all. He now commands us to ready to do the same. He wants us to love each other including our enemies. We must work hard to build these bridges.

This is a difficult command to follow. We may say that we can do this, but we must really search our hearts to see if we have that strong a faith. Pray that you are that kind of Christian that beyond self you will obey Jesus.

*DAY 2*
*SUGGESTED READING*
*1 JOHN 4:19 - 21*

**[19] We love because he first loved us.**

**[20] Whoever claims to love God yet hates a brother or sister is a liar. For whoever does not love their brother and sister, whom they have seen, cannot love God, whom they have not seen.**

**[21] And he has given us this command: Anyone who loves God must also love their brother and sister. (NIV)**

I find it interesting that there are religions out there that will not share their faith by reaching out to others. I also find it horrifying that there are religions out there that will kill you if you don't subscribe to their dogma. Where is the love in these religions? How does one establish relationships with those that are a closed group or with those that you fear for your life if you do not agree?

God reached out to us with love. We accepted. We built a relationship with Him. We as Christians are compelled to do the same with everyone. Reach out with love. The relationships will build.

DAY 3
SUGGESTED READING
1 CORINTHIANS 13:13

**[13] And now these three remain: faith, hope and love. But the greatest of these is love. (NIV)**

To establish any relationship a foundation is necessary. Paul puts love first in as the foundation. Without love, faith and hope are suspect. Faith without love leaves room for suspicion. Hope without love is more like a wish. There is no basis to think hope will abide.

We started our relationship with God on the understanding that he loved us. We grew to love him through study of the Bible, fellowship with other Christians and understanding the gospel and sacrifice of Christ.

We start our relationships with our fellow man with the same love that God has given to us. As our relationship builds so does our faith and hope for its future.

*DAY 4*
*SUGGESTED READING*
*EPHESIANS 6:1 - 3*

**¹Children, obey your parents in the Lord, for this is right.**

**² "Honor your father and mother"—which is the first commandment with a promise—**

**³ "so that it may go well with you and that you may enjoy long life on the earth." (NIV)**

It is the parents job to raise their children with a solid foundation of faith in God. Children should be taught from an early age. They should be involved in church and be involved in family prayer.

It is also important for children to learn how to love others. They should not be taught prejudice but how the love of God is equal to everyone.

In return, children should listen and obey their parents. This should be a natural process as they see their parents as God fairing role models. The reverence should be internal and external that their love is obvious to all.

DAY 5
SUGGESTED READING
2 CORINTHIANS 6:14

**¹⁴ Do not be yoked together with unbelievers. For what do righteousness and wickedness have in common? Or what fellowship can light have with darkness? (NIV)**

There is a contrast between the righteous and the lawless. Each do things differently. The first with the Holy Spirit guiding one's thoughts and behavior, the second with Satan's guidance.

Paul warns us against alliances between the two. There are different philosophies which are inconsistent with each other. Where the sinner has nothing to lose with such a collaboration, the believer has everything to lose. There is elevated risk of falling into sin when working with the lawless. Sometimes it is unavoidable to not have relationships with sinners. In these cases, we must be careful to maintain our faith and not follow their lead. We should never compromise our Christian standards for Man.

*DAY 6*
*SUGGESTED READING*
*EPHESIANS 4:2 - 3*

**² Be completely humble and gentle; be patient, bearing with one another in love.**

**³ Make every effort to keep the unity of the Spirit through the bond of peace. (NIV)**

Relationships are difficult to cultivate and maintain. They require continuous effort. We are all difference and want to enforce our own will. So, we must make extra effort in being accepting of others points of view.

Paul reminds us of how Jesus builds relationships. We need to stay connected with the Holy Spirit and be as Jesus. We must strive to love one another.

DAY 7
SUGGESTED READING
ROMANS 12:16

**¹⁶ Live in harmony with one another. Do not be proud but be willing to associate with people of low position. Do not be conceited. (NIV)**

A trap of Satan is pride. Christians are very proud of being Christian and tell everyone about it. This is a dangerous situation though. Because of this pride, one can start to belief that they are better than unbelievers or even those who they perceive to have lesser faith.

Focus on God's love for all. Have this in our hearts and we can build relationships with all equally. Love will eliminate the superficial worldly circumstance of someone and reveal their inner spirit. This puts everyone on a level playing field.

# WEEK 50
# TEMPTATION

DAY 1
SUGGESTED READING
1 CORINTHIANS 10:13

**¹³ No temptation has overtaken you except what is common to mankind. And God is faithful; he will not let you be tempted beyond what you can bear. But when you are tempted, he will also provide a way out so that you can endure it. (NIV)**

Temptation is a part of worldly life. Believer and non-believer alike is subject to its calling. This is Satan's mission to lead us away from God. There are times when we feel that our temptation is unique but even this is not the case. All temptation has happened before and is common.

God tells us that he will not present a temptation that is not within our power to overcome. God knows that we are not sinless. He knows our breaking point. He uses these temptations as lessons for us to grow spiritually. He will not let them ruin us.

*DAY 2*
*SUGGESTED READING*
*JAMES 1:12*

**¹² Blessed is the one who perseveres under trial because, having stood the test, that person will receive the crown of life that the Lord has promised to those who love him. (NIV)**

In reality, temptations are trials that we endure through life. The trials can have either beneficial outcomes or disastrous outcomes depending on how one responds to the temptation.

A temptation is not a sin of itself, but surely can lead to sin. We, as Christians, must look at all temptation with our spiritual eye and determine if it is something not consistent with the nature of God. If not, we must deny ourselves the sinful desire.

God knows we are not perfect and will not resist all temptation, but with each trial comes the chance for spiritual growth. Pray for strength to get through the trials. Pray for forgiveness and repent when you come up short. The Lord is with you either way.

DAY 3
SUGGESTED READING
MATTHEW 26:41

> **⁴¹ Watch and pray, that ye enter not into temptation: the spirit indeed is willing, but the flesh is weak. (KJV)**

Temptation varies according to the weakness of each person. What is easy for some to resist is very difficult for others. Though temptation is not evil it can lead to solicitations of evil. The outcomes depend on how a person responds to the temptation.

We must always be vigilant of temptation. We can't always rely on our ability to overcome every situation. Our power to resist comes from God through prayer. He is all powerful and will help us endure.

*DAY 4*
*SUGGESTED READING*
*JAMES 1:13*

**¹³ When tempted, no one should say, "God is tempting me." For God cannot be tempted by evil, nor does he tempt anyone; (NIV)**

No one can say that God has tempted him. To blame God shows a complete misunderstanding of the nature of God. When sin is involved in temptation it no longer is something related to God. Sin begins in our hearts and mind and grow as the temptation strengthens. It is easier for one to blame someone else for their sinful desires than to accept responsibility themselves.

Spending time in study and prayer are the most important actions to understanding the nature of God and resisting temptation. If our hearts and mind are in the right place, then so will be our response to temptation.

DAY 5
SUGGESTED READING
GALATIANS 6:1

**¹Brothers and sisters, if someone is caught in a sin, you who live by the Spirit should restore that person gently. But watch yourselves, or you also may be tempted. (NIV)**

It is our mission to spread the gospel of Christ. Part of this gospel is to recognize sin and share the burden with the affected in an attempt to restore them. When we see someone that is succumbing to the temptations of the world, we spiritually obligated to help them.

These efforts can take time as bringing them back in line with the righteous way must be done with patience and gentleness. The danger in spending the time and getting to understand the temptation can put the helper at risk also. Bearing the burden of someone else's sin is not as easy as problems of physical nature. Sin is spiritual and always begins with temptation.

*DAY 6*
*SUGGESTED READING*
*MATTHEW 6:13*

## ¹³ And lead us not into temptation, but deliver us from the evil one (NIV)

This is a prayer for strength in the face of temptations trials. The temptations are not of God but of Satan. Satan wants to direct us away from God by any means and tempts us with the seven deadly sins: Lust, Gluttony, Greed, Sloth, Wrath, Envy, Pride.

God will allow trials in our lives to strengthen our faith. He causes the trials that accompany temptation and allows us to suffer under its pressure. These trials will never be more than we can manage for all temptation is under His control. This is why we pray for God to sustain us. He will get us through these trying times and our faith is stronger as a result.

DAY 7
SUGGESTED READING
HEBREWS 4:15

**[15] For we do not have a high priest who is unable to empathize with our weaknesses, but we have one who has been tempted in every way, just as we are—yet he did not sin. (NIV)**

The Word of God came to us in the form a man. This man was Jesus. He experienced everything man goes through on a daily basis. He experienced joy and experienced sorrow. He was subject to the temptations of Satan just as we are.

Jesus had choices when he was a man. Though he was exposed to many hardships, he chose to trust in God. Jesus set the example for all us to follow. He chose not to give in to temptation and sin.

# WEEK 51
# PARABLES

## DAY 1
## SUGGESTED READING
## MATTHEW 7:24 - 27

**²⁴ "Therefore everyone who hears these words of mine and puts them into practice is like a wise man who built his house on the rock.**

**²⁵ The rain came down, the streams rose, and the winds blew and beat against that house; yet it did not fall, because it had its foundation on the rock.**

**²⁶ But everyone who hears these words of mine and does not put them into practice is like a foolish man who built his house on sand.**

**²⁷ The rain came down, the streams rose, and the winds blew and beat against that house, and it fell with a great crash." (NIV)**

Solomon tells us, "By wisdom a house is built, and by understanding it is established." (Proverbs 24:3 NIV). As this is true for our house it is true for our life. This parable tells the importance of understanding the Word of God and using this knowledge as our foundation.

It also warns of the opposite. Without the knowledge God we put our lives in peril. As with a house built on a weak foundation, our lives are at elevated risk of failure. Jesus explains that this is the difference between the wise and the foolish.

DAY 2
SUGGESTED READING
MATTHEW 12:43

**⁴³ "When an impure spirit comes out of a person, it goes through arid places seeking rest and does not find it. (NIV)**

Jesus talks about the state of evil in man. He states that once evil is removed from our soul it has no place to go.

This does not make us immune to evil as it is not destroyed. It is just displaced for a time. If we are not careful it can come back. Replace the former sinful nature with righteousness. Old behaviors must be stopped, and new ones must be put in place. Evil cannot return to inhabit your soul if you keep God in your life.

DAY 3
SUGGESTED READING
MATTHEW 13:3

**³ And he spake many things unto them in parables, saying, Behold, a sower went forth to sow; (KJV)**

Jesus uses parables to get his message across. He did not just state a fact or doctrine but used imagery to implant the lesson with relatable events. All his parables had a moral foundation. Most of the time he would use these as teaching tools to his disciples, but this is the first time that he spoke to the masses in parables.

The purpose of his parable teaching was to convey truth in a more interesting manner, to teach spiritual truth, to rebuke in a way to appeal to the conscience and to conceal the message from a portion of audience while revealing the truths to those intended.

*DAY 4*
*SUGGESTED READING*
*MATTHEW 13:35*

## **[35] So was fulfilled what was spoken through the prophet:**

## **"I will open my mouth in parables, I will utter things hidden since the creation of the world." (NIV)**

Jesus explains that the parables will be used to explain things that have not been discussed or revealed since the beginning of the world. These things were hidden because they were of Satanic origin.

Jesus wanted these secrets known so he gives this knowledge to his disciples (those who believe and follow him) for them to share with the masses.

DAY 5
SUGGESTED READING
MATTHEW 13:10 - 11

**[10] The disciples came to him and asked, "Why do you speak to the people in parables?"**

**[11] He replied, "Because the knowledge of the secrets of the kingdom of heaven has been given to you, but not to them. (NIV)**

The disciples did not realize that they were favored among all. This included the prophets of old. They were favored because they were in the presence of Jesus. As such they were privy to information that was not available to any in Earth's history.

The knowledge that Jesus gave them was the understanding of the parables that he delivered to the masses. This knowledge was for only the most advanced disciples and it was charged to them to teach everyone else.

*DAY 6*
*SUGGESTED READING*
*JOHN 10:6*

> **⁶ This parable spake Jesus unto them: but they understood not what things they were which he spake unto them. (KJV)**

Speaking parables to the Pharisees had them confused. This was because they were not committed to Jesus's message from God. When they reject this message anything Jesus tried to teach them was incomprehensible. "'You will be ever hearing but never understanding; you will be ever seeing but never perceiving." (Matthew 13:14 NIV)

In contrast, those who are committed to the message of God through Jesus will understand the meaning of the parables through study and meditation.

DAY 7
SUGGESTED READING
MARK 4:34

**³⁴ He did not say anything to them without using a parable. But when he was alone with his own disciples, he explained everything. (NIV)**

Not all understand the parables of Jesus. Even his disciples had difficulty with complete understanding. This intentional confusion inspired many to seek answers, so they would seek out the disciples. It was true then and remains true today.

Jesus is not here to teach us today. We have his word though. The Bible gives us explanation to all the parables Jesus taught by. We are armed with the same understanding that was given to the disciples. Read and reread the parables with prayer for understanding that we may use them in our sharing of the gospel of Christ.

# WEEK 52
# ABOUT HELL

*DAY 1*
*SUGGESTED READING*
*REVELATION 21:8*

> **⁸ But the cowardly, the unbelieving, the vile, the murderers, the sexually immoral, those who practice magic arts, the idolaters and all liars—they will be consigned to the fiery lake of burning sulfur. This is the second death." (NIV)**

It is understood that once we have died we will be risen at the day of judgement. For the believer they shall enjoy the blessing of God and reside with him forever with eternal life. But for the unbeliever, their fate is the second death.

There is no worse fate that can happen to man. This is the fate that is promised for those that are disobedient to God's law. There is no coming back after this judgement.

DAY 2
SUGGESTED READING
REVELATION 14:10 - 11

**¹⁰ they, too, will drink the wine of God's fury, which has been poured full strength into the cup of his wrath. They will be tormented with burning sulfur in the presence of the holy angels and of the Lamb.**

**¹¹ And the smoke of their torment will rise for ever and ever. There will be no rest day or night for those who worship the beast and its image, or for anyone who receives the mark of its name." (NIV)**

The metaphor here reminds the sinner that they have spent their lives drinking the wine of sinful things. For their disobedience God now promises the fullness of his wrath. This is without dilution or holding back.

To make matters worse, this wrath is not temporary. It is a torment that is continuous and last forever. This God promises to the followers of Satan.

DAY 3
SUGGESTED READING
MATTHEW 25:46

**⁴⁶ "Then they will go away to eternal punishment, but the righteous to eternal life." (NIV)**

We are to understand that once we are judged, the sentence is final. There is no appeal process that can follow. The sentence is forever as sin is now a part of their eternal soul. This will never be acceptable in the Kingdom of God.

But for those who have dedicated their lives to good principles and avoidance of sin will have the blessing of eternal life. Their labors on Earth are promised by God.

*DAY 4*
*SUGGESTED READING*
*2 THESSALONIANS 1:9*

**⁹ They will be punished with everlasting destruction and shut out from the presence of the Lord and from the glory of his might (NIV)**

Being cast into Hell is more than being tormented forever. The lost souls will never have access to God and will be forever ignored by God. For those who never believed that there was a God will then know the errors of their ways.

The presence of the Lord is love. His followers will experience his glory and power forever. Not being in the presence of the Lord removes any chance of being happy at any time. There will be no relief from pain ever. "In that place there will be weeping and gnashing of teeth" (Matthew 13:50 ESV)

DAY 5
SUGGESTED READING
REVELATION 20:13 - 15

> **¹³ The sea gave up the dead that were in it, and death and Hades gave up the dead that were in them, and each person was judged according to what they had done.**
>
> **¹⁴ Then death and Hades were thrown into the lake of fire. The lake of fire is the second death.**
>
> **¹⁵ Anyone whose name was not found written in the book of life was thrown into the lake of fire. (NIV)**

Understand that once the unbeliever dies they are placed in a temporary Hell until judgement. Though their physical bodies are dead and wasted away, their souls remain. At the time of judgement, the angels are sent forth and everyone is collected and brought before God for final judgement.

God reviews their life choices and determines their fate. He judges based on the type of life one has led. That being said eternal life is a gift of God. It is not based on the deeds of someone. Though your deeds do not affect your salvation status, they surely can condemn you. Living a life of sin and disbelief will not earn you a spot in the Book of Life and if one is not in the Book of Life they will be cast into the Lake of Fire.

All who were in the temporary Hell will be cast into the Lake of Fire which is eternal. This is the second death. It is the complete and final separation from God. The concept is simple: if you are born once, you will die twice, if you are born twice, you will die once. This is the most important concept that you can share with the non-believer.

DAY 6
SUGGESTED READING
MATTHEW 13:49

**⁴⁹ So shall it be at the end of the world: the angels shall come forth, and sever the wicked from among the just,**

**⁵⁰ And shall cast them into the furnace of fire: there shall be wailing and gnashing of teeth. (KJV)**

At the time of judgement God will send out the angels to gather all souls of man who have died throughout time and all man living on that day. The angels will sort out the sinners from the righteous.

The judgement to the sinner would get them cast into Hell. There can be no greater sorrow for these wretched people and souls who now know that they chose incorrectly in their life choices.

DAY 7
SUGGESTED READING
MATTHEW 10:28

**²⁸ And fear not them which kill the body but are not able to kill the soul: but rather fear him which is able to destroy both soul and body in hell. (KJV)**

The world is evil. Christians are constantly being subjected to hate and violence internationally. Many have given their lives for God. Nonetheless, we must persevere. We must live according to the Word of God and trust that He has our best interest at heart.

Man can only kill us once and that involves only our physical bodies. Our soul remains which Satan has no dominion over. Though it is a difficult concept because death is typically accompanied by pain, we should not fear it. We must believe with all our heart that we will overcome this physical death.

What we must be afraid of is death caused by God. When God kills, he separates our soul from his presence and cast it into Hell. There is no coming back from a death by God. This is what we should fear because it is permanent. This is the second and final death of which there is no resurrection.